Soul Choices

Six Paths to Find Your Life Purpose

Kathryn Andries

INTUITIVE
ARTS PRESS

Intuitive Arts Press
Palatine, Illinois

INTUITIVE
ARTS PRESS

P.O. Box 2071
Palatine, IL 60078

Copyright 2003 by Kathryn Andries

Printed in the United States of America.

ISBN 0-9741334-0-X
Library of Congress Catalogue Number 2003106525

Cover design by Debbie Mackall

Layout design and interior art by Patrick Andries

I dedicate this book to my family for providing me with love and a solid foundation that enabled me to find my life purpose.

ENDORSEMENTS

"*Soul Choices* captures your spirit and takes you on a mystical adventure to find your life purpose."

> — Linda Cole, CSP, professional speaker and writer

"A tribute to the divine and complex nature of the Universe! Kathryn teaches us how to use astrology in conjunction with other forms of self-awareness to understand all aspects of ourselves. This book will stretch your intellect to go beyond the traditional routes to create a satisfying life."

> —Michelle Gobely, Astrologer, MAFA, teacher for the American Federation of Astrologers

"*Soul Choices* brilliantly demonstrates how to use Spiritual/Emotional Iridology to discover your life purpose. The eyes truly are the window to the soul and you'll get a glimpse of the incredible amount of knowledge to be discovered about yourself from the interpretation of your iris patterns as you read this book. Great job!"

> — Dave Carpenter, N.D., L.AC, V.P., International Iridology Practitioners Association

"*Soul Choices* offers highly useful tools for beginning the journey of Self understanding."

> — Susan Wisehart, past life regression therapist and holistic psychotherapist

Contents

Foreward

I dream of a world where everyone knows—and lives—their life purpose. I know how to make this happen and I want to share it with you.

I knew at a very young age that I was here to fulfill an important mission. Neither school nor work helped me discover this mission. So, I began to search in other directions.

It was no accident that my family practiced no formal religion, thereby giving me the freedom to explore many spiritual avenues. During my years of spiritual study, I learned that I chose the major influences in my life, from my family to my time of birth. In seeking to understand why I chose these particular influences, I discovered my life purpose.

At the age of 12, I began to read books on spirituality, everything from Edgar Cayce to Ruth Montgomery. Theories about reincarnation and Universal Laws resonated with me. From books, I moved on to consulting psychics and healers. I had my palm read and began transcendental meditation. Each book and teacher brought me closer to unlocking my life purpose and led me to the next step on my journey.

In my late 20s, an astrologer helped me learn the cause of many of my behaviors, including why I chose particular relationships. Astrology proved to be an important part of the puzzle that I was beginning to piece together.

I could also turn to my body to reveal more self-knowledge. I studied mind-body therapies at Body Mind College in California. I learned how everything about my body—from the way I held my shoulders to the way I walked—reflected my thoughts. I experimented with various healing modalities, from herbs to homeopathy to emotional release methods such as rebirthing. I was amazed at the way these bioenergetic forms of healing could shift my mental, emotional, and physical states.

My interest in health led me to iridology and Rayid iris (two fascinating studies of the eyes). The eyes—the proverbial "windows to the soul"—contain a wealth of knowledge on physical, mental, and emotional levels. My eyes revealed my health and personality—a complete mind-body picture.

At the Berkeley Psychic Institute, I began to develop nonphysical healing methods as well as my intuitive abilities. I learned to connect with my spirit guides and use energy to heal myself and others.

While attending a health fair, I discovered the School of Metaphysics, through which I explored the inner workings of the mind and the Universal Laws. I learned how to interpret my dreams and go deeper in my meditation practices. I explored intuitive reports, retrieved from the Akashic Library, detailing past lives that I shared with family, friends, and lovers. These reports offered profound lessons and excellent guidance.

Arriving (finally!) at a point in my quest where I had gathered all the pieces I could find, I reflected. "Would I be further along in my path if I had been able to access this information at a younger age? Would others benefit from this information? What if all this information were available in one source?"

In answer to these questions, I wrote this book to offer a structure and a path for those seeking their life purpose. Only by becoming self-aware can we learn what that purpose is. *Soul Choices* guides the reader through six remarkable approaches to developing self-awareness and revealing the choices our souls have made. By synthesizing the information gleaned from these approaches, readers will be able to come up with a life purpose statement.

I recognize the beauty of each person's journey and do not wish to diminish the splendor of the discovery process by mapping out everything in this book. Rather, I hope this book will serve to give the reader guidance and encouragement to start—and remain steadfast—on the path to self-awareness and unlocking life's purpose. I wish you well on your journey.

Kathryn Andries

One

Choices of the Soul: Finding Purpose

Well before we were born, our souls—the eternal, permanent part of us that incarnates into a physical body—made choices that greatly impact our lives. By understanding why our souls chose as they did, we can discover our life purpose.

Many of us have not found our purpose because we rely only on the conscious mind for answers. We have distanced ourselves from what our souls deeply desire. As children, we were still in close contact with our souls. We expressed our life purpose through the activities we enjoyed, the games we played, our artwork, and the fantasy worlds we created.

As we grew older, we shut down communication with our inner selves—our subconscious—forgetting our purpose and relying more on our conscious mind and the desires of other people. Responding to our conscious desires may fulfill us, but only temporarily. Eventually we feel empty and bored because we are not responding to the soul's desires—our life purpose.

There are many ways to bring us closer to our soul, such as through meditation and journaling. This book offers additional avenues—six approaches—to connect us with our soul and help us discover our life purpose: past lives, astrology, numerology, Rayid iris, palmistry, and family and birth order. Each approach reveals our karma, as well as our gifts and talents, all needed to piece together our life mission. Each time we master a lesson, gain new wisdom, or share our gifts and talents, we embody more of our potential greatness.

PRELUDE TO THE JOURNEY

Since we are the culmination of our past lives (which have led us to this point in our evolution), we will begin before the current incarnation with a look into past lives and reincarnation. The book then moves to the time of our birth and examines the planetary configurations through astrology.

Next, we will look at the numerological configurations present at the time of our birth. The names our parents chose for us also reveal much about who we can become. Through our eyes, we will enter a doorway to understanding our inner urges, desires, gifts, and talents.

The shape of our hands and their lines form a map of our potential destiny in the areas of health, career, and love.

The family provides our first arena for learning. Souls choose a family based on the learning opportunities they offer. By examining our familial environment and all the players involved, we can understand our karma.

We will then learn how to organize the self-awareness information gathered to extract repeated lessons, strengths, and weaknesses. We will synthesize this information to formulate a life purpose. We will go through the process of how to master lessons to accelerate our soul growth. In the final stage of this journey, we will learn to implement and live our life purpose, and change old, limiting patterns of thinking, replacing them with attitudes that engender growth and happiness.

PRINCIPLES OF THE LIFE PURPOSE METHOD

Choice
The first and most important of the principles that form the foundation of the life purpose method is choice. We choose everything in life that will help us fulfill our mission.

Free Will
Free will, the most powerful influence in the universe, can override any other influence.

Karmic Lessons and Gifts

Life purpose is achieved by mastering karmic lessons and by developing gifts and talents. Lessons not mastered become stumbling blocks to using gifts and talents. As we build our gifts and talents, we encounter lessons to be learned.

Familiarity

Familiar influences are those already developed and understood through experiences from past lives. They give us a foundation of talents requiring little effort to bring out. To develop new understandings, we choose unfamiliar influences. They may be challenging at first, but experience will help us make these understandings permanent additions to our soul.

Positive and Negative

Every influence has both positive and negative forms of expression. Influences themselves are neutral; since we have free will, we choose the vibrational expression. For example, in astrology, the planet Neptune urges us to identify and develop our spiritual selves. We can use this energy in a positive way to make great strides in spiritual development or choose the destructive path of drugs and alcohol as a way to escape our troubles. This book identifies the higher and lower expressions of each influence so that you can choose with awareness at every moment.

Opposites Attract

In astrology, each zodiacal sign has an opposite. In numerology, each number is the vibrational opposite of the number preceding it. Of the four iris types and palm shapes, there are two pairs of opposites. The polarities between opposites create a strong pull because they hold lessons for us.

To attain balance, we must often develop the qualities of our opposite. In a mate, these qualities may heighten passion, intensity, and learning potential.

The Power of 3, 4, and 6

The numbers 3 and 4 have significant vibrations: "3" is the number of self-expression, "4" of stability. "4" also represents the building of a foundation. Through 3's vibration, we find out who we are. We use 4's stability to build the foundation of our identity.

These numbers recur throughout the six approaches. In palmistry, there are four major palm shapes. In astrology, we speak of four elements and three qualities or modes. There are also three main players: the planets, the 12 (4 x 3) zodiac signs, and the 12 houses. Rayid iris comprises four principal iris structures. Numerology uses three numbers to calculate core numbers (date, month, and year of birth). Most numerological cycles are made up of four periods; there are four challenge numbers. Letters of the alphabet fall into four planes of existence (physical, mental, spiritual, intuitive) and three qualities (creative, vacillating, grounded). Our lives progress in cycles of nine (3 x 3). Within the family unit, your mother, your father, and you form a triad.

There are six major influences. The number "6" concerns service to humanity. When we incorporate our gifts and talents from the six approaches, we can offer the greatest service to the world.

Energy

Energy is the link among all the approaches to self-awareness. To understand how these influences affect us and how we use them, we need to understand the nature of energy. Einstein told us that "Energy can neither be created nor destroyed, it simply changes form." Energy is always in motion.

The Universe is a pulsating energy field where everything is in motion, from the tiniest atom to the skyscrapers that line our city skies. Most things appear solid to us because we perceive only a portion of what exists. Every person, plant, animal, and object is surrounded by a vibrating field of energy: the aura. Auras reflect our thoughts and attitudes, which emit a powerful vibration that shapes our lives.

The influences described by the six approaches in this book affect us through vibrating energy, which determines how we perceive the world and what we do with our lives. Wisdom attained during past lifetimes remains within our souls as a vibrating source of knowledge. Astrologically, we experience vibrations from various planets. Each number emits vibrations based on its unique characteristics. Patterns in our eyes and hands also vibrate with influences that shape our personality. Vibrations of the souls of our family members and other partners draw us to them.

To effectively live our life purpose we must be in harmony with these energetic vibrations. When we understand any or all of the six approaches in this book, we can learn to harmonize with their energetic qualities, align ourselves with our life purpose, and be masters of energy rather than victims.

Many of us experience this energy as urges or desires. Indeed, that is how the soul speaks to us. If we allow ourselves to follow these urges, most of them will lead us to lessons and experiences that will enrich our soul. When I follow my heart's desires, I feel fulfilled and experience exuberant health. Suppression of—whether thoughts or desires— causes our energy to be misdirected, leading to imbalances such as depression and illness.

From Exhaustion to Energy

As much as I enjoyed teaching, my passion eventually moved to health and healing. I was still teaching second grade when I opened a holistic health practice. After a day of teaching, I was often exhausted. On the drive to the office, thinking about my new career slowly brought back my energy. By the end of my 30-minute ride, I was enthusiastic and ready to see as many as three to four clients.

I continued this schedule for three months, when I transitioned into a full-time healing practice. I experienced firsthand how abundant energy can be when we tap into our desires, do what we love, and align ourselves with our life purpose.

Potential

Even the most challenging energies offer the greatest opportunity to evolve. Through self-awareness we can use such challenging influences—as well as gifts and talents—productively to fulfill our life purpose. We must keep in mind that all influences describe our potential. Choosing the higher vibration affords us unlimited potential. It is up to us to fulfill that potential.

We can think of our lives as a path that weaves its way through these influences. To reach our destination—fulfilling our life purpose—in a timely and productive way, we need to be aware of the influences along the road. When obstacles crop up, delaying or detouring us, we can see where we are out of harmony with our influences and realign ourselves with our life purpose.

Soul Choices will bring us to a higher level of awareness and self-acceptance, and make it easier to trust our inner guidance. Those of us determined to find our life purpose will no longer depend on outside sources for answers. We will become our own teachers and the masters of our destiny.

When we use all these approaches to self-awareness to the fullest, we can aspire to live in alignment with our life purpose. We will have more to give to ourselves and to others. If we fail to use these tools, we will not only go through life mostly unaware of our purpose, but we will have missed a great opportunity to learn about ourselves.

We are divine souls, each with unique gifts and talents to share. No two souls have followed the same path. May this book lead you to appreciate the journey you have led and the person you have become.

WHY SHOULD YOU FIND YOUR LIFE PURPOSE?

As you read and work through the processes in this book, keep in mind the following benefits of finding your life purpose:

1. Increase self-awareness. *Each approach reveals more about your inner self.*
2. Discover your gifts, talents, and karmic lessons. *These are the components you'll need to create and realize your desires and fulfill your life purpose.*
3. Improve relationships with others. *Take responsibility for your issues. Recognize and cooperate with others' influences.*
4. Move through lessons and challenges with confidence. *Gain new insight into your inner conflicts. Learn how your influences affect your karma.*
5. Achieve mental, emotional, and physical harmony. *Get in tune with your energies.*
6. Fall in love with yourself. *There will be more about you to admire as you increase your self-knowledge and surmount challenges.*
7. Become the master of your life. *Put your influences to work and reach your potential.*

HOW TO USE THIS BOOK

This book outlines a journey; it is up to each of us how far we are willing to travel. It is not intended to make you an expert in the approaches to self-awareness presented, which require in-depth study and experience. To receive the most accurate information possible, I recommend that you consult experienced practitioners.

To reap the full benefits of this book—reaching full self-awareness and finding life's purpose—it is important to perform the tasks, answer the questions, and do the exercises at the end of each chapter before continuing to the next chapter. I also encourage you to read and work through this book with a friend or with a group. You will learn from others' processes as much as your own, with the added benefit—and fun—of mutual support and sharing. Your support group can offer insights and guidance as you progress, often noticing things in you that you may not be aware of. A group also provides a wonderful opportunity for networking and sharing resources.

Do the tasks first, keeping in mind the questions as guideposts. Most of the tasks will require finding a practitioner in the various approaches to self-analysis described. I have listed several references to help you do this. If you are unable to get in touch with any of the practitioners listed, check other resources such as health food stores, metaphysical bookstores, alternative healers, meditation groups, your local library, and, of course, the Internet. Your thoughts and intentions are powerful, so have faith that you will attract knowledgeable teachers in these fields of self-development.

The questions and the exercises are designed to help you gain—and enhance—a deeper understanding of yourself. Build on what you have learned from the tasks by doing the exercises. You may wish to record your answers to the questions and exercises in a notebook or binder. You can also include a transcription of your past life profiles, past life regression sessions, astrology and numerology charts, iris photos, palm photos, family photos and past life family readings, memoirs from significant relationships, and any other information you collect along the way. Use this record of your path to understanding your life purpose to hold and treasure your newfound awareness and learning. Be creative: design a cover that reflects your personality, style, and life purpose.

If you work with a group, think about having a book-decorating-and-sharing party. Enjoy!

TIP: You may want to read all the tasks in the book first so that you can search for practitioners and set up appointments ahead of time to avoid lag time between chapters.

Two

Reincarnation: Influences from the Past

Freedom or Responsibility?

Elaine was a wife and mother of three, struggling to understand how to fulfill her desire for freedom and still be responsible. Through a past life profile, Elaine gained new perspective.

She lived in Japan. In the year 400, when she was 12, she joined a group of women whose duty (neither religion based nor sexually oriented) was to take care of men. Her father decided that she was to dedicate her life to this service, which was seen as an honor. She, however, was torn between the opportunity to serve and feeling trapped. She was reprimanded when she offered her thoughts and ideas. With growing discontent, she finally escaped and lived in isolation so as not to dishonor her family. At the end of her life, she felt that she had not accomplished what she was meant to do.

Elaine recognized the parallel to her current lifetime. She often felt that she was no more than a caretaker for her husband, always trying to please him, as she had done in Japan more than 1,600 years ago. Although she enjoyed motherhood, she still wanted other avenues to express her creativity. The report stated that she needed to see free-

9

dom and responsibility as one and the same, that true free-
dom lies in the ability to respond to situations any way
one chooses.

She began to recognize and appreciate the opportunities
in her life. To give herself an avenue to express her cre-
ativity, she enrolled in an interior design course. She then
sought the guidance of a marriage counselor, who helped
her gain greater self-confidence to make her own deci-
sions. Since she was no longer hindered by low self-es-
teem, she felt the freedom to make beneficial decisions for
herself.

Elaine began to take steps to explore spirituality, which
her husband often ridiculed as a waste of time. Not allow-
ing him to hold her back, she attended a five-day spiritual
retreat at the Light Institute in New Mexico. She nour-
ished her soul with past life regressions, meditation, and
spiritual conversations.

As she exercised her choices, Elaine's fulfillment grew. She
now understands that freedom comes from having enough
self-confidence to make satisfying life choices.

Our souls occupy a physical body on Earth to gain wisdom in order to reach our
highest potential. We began incarnating into bodies during the time of Atlantis, some
60,000 to 70,000 years ago. Since then, most of us have averaged about 100 lifetimes. Is it possible to learn everything in one lifetime? If it were, we would not
continue to reincarnate into the physical world lifetime after lifetime.

The theory of reincarnation originated in the East where it is an integral part of
life, where death is celebrated as a step forward for the soul. It is based on the
premise that we continue to reincarnate on the Earth plane until we have fulfilled our karma. In the late 1800s, theosophists introduced this concept to the
West. In the 1940s, Edgar Cayce began doing past life readings, demonstrating
that reincarnation was possible.

Within each lifetime we accumulate karma. Karma comprises the lessons and awareness we need to complete our learning on the physical plane. Karma brings balance,
insuring that our good deeds will be rewarded, and that our bad deeds will be recti-
fied by understanding. Each soul chooses to be born rich or poor, in good health or
bad, to achieve its highest learning potential. Until all the karma is relieved through
the understanding gleaned from the lessons, we will continue learning in the physi-

cal plane. With free will, we can accept or reject any lesson that comes our way. If we reject a lesson it will return to us later, slowing our development and growth.

We create karma by intention. Identical acts by two people may result in different karma for each based on their intentions. A soldier in the midst of battle kills an enemy soldier in self-defense. A thief kills a bank teller to avoid identification in court. In both instances, someone took a life, yet because their intentions were dissimilar, different lessons lie ahead for each of them.

Examining the karma we developed in past lives helps us understand the choices our soul made for this life. Souls choose family, period, place and date of birth, and gender based on what offers the greatest opportunity for learning. A past life in which you abused your freedom may explain why you were born in a communist country, with no personal freedom. Perhaps, generous in a past lifetime, you were born into a rich family with many privileges in this lifetime.

One way to obtain past life information is through spontaneous recall. This is usually triggered by an event, person, or object. For example, a visit to a battle site may trigger a flood of memories from a past life as a soldier. Meeting your husband from a previous lifetime can cause a flood of emotion and love to well up inside you, leaving you feeling that you have known this person before. Rebirthing, an emotional release therapy, can also cause people to have a spontaneous recall of a prior lifetime.

Another way to retrieve past life information is through a disciplined mind—one able to quiet the conscious mind and move within to the subconscious mind. One such mind was Edgar Cayce (1877–1945), who was known as the "sleeping prophet" because he was able to put his conscious mind to sleep and retrieve past life information for individuals through his subconscious mind.

The School of Metaphysics offers past life profiles, accessed and reported by a team of two people, the conductor and the intuitive reporter. (A past life crossing report, also available, describes a lifetime shared by two people, making a connection between past and present interactions.) The conductor leads the intuitive reporter into a trance-like state where the conscious mind is asleep, then repeats the name of the person requesting the profile.

Based on the vibration of the requester's name, the reporter accesses and relates only the past life that is most pertinent to the present one. This is usually a lifetime where the requester held similar thoughts and attitudes. The report reveals detailed information about the past life, the period, the country, and the requester's name in that life. It then explains the significance of the past life experiences to the present. This key to growth allows us to see the similarities in karma so that we can learn and evolve beyond the past lifetime. Otherwise, we would repeat the same mistakes and impose on ourselves the same limitations that slow the growth of our soul.

The records of our past lives are stored in the Akashic Library, a nonphysical compilation of every thought, deed, and action of every soul since the beginning of time. Limitations can often turn into problems. Information from a past life—accessing wisdom from the Akashic records—may hold the key to solving these problems. Einstein believed that "A problem cannot be solved at the level it was created."

Another way to access past life information is through past life regression therapy. A facilitator trained in hypnotherapy, perhaps with a background in psychology or psychiatry, puts the requester under hypnosis using relaxation techniques, guided visualization, and certain words or phrases. The facilitator then directs her to the area of focus. A person may choose any type of focus for the session, such as understanding the root of a trauma, a lesson he is now encountering, or the reason she is drawn to a particular country. Once in this alpha state, the subject can access key information to initiate deep healing.

Everyone has different experiences during a past life regression session. Some observe the past life; others relive it. Past lives may be experienced as images or as sensory impressions. Past life regression may help release pent-up feelings, break patterns, and reveal addictions. Through past life regression, we see the existence of the soul—separate from our body—and that we are eternal. By becoming aware of the consequences of our actions, we see the realization of karma: our life is the result of cumulative intentions and actions.

A past life regression requires the ability to relax and be hypnotized. If you have little practice with meditation and other relaxation techniques, consider having a trained Akashic record reader do your reading first.

Following is an example of an Akashic record reading for "Kathleen."

> *We see this one in female form. We see this land area to be that referred to as Denmark. We see this one to have had difficulty within the audible faculties of the physical body; this one was unable to produce sound. We see however this one was able to use the other senses to a great extent.*

We see that this one was very quick minded and we see therefore at a very young age, this one was able to communicate through the written word. ...

We see for this one to be very talented in word and very descriptive with this one's thoughts for we see that this one did absorb within the self all that this one could and we see this one did desire to teach other individuals. We see that at first that this one did gravitate to others that had difficulties that this one did physically, however, we see that this one eventually placed the self in types of environments where the children were very well cared for and were very well educated. We see that this one at first did feel intimidated by this experience; however, we see that through this one's genuineness and love that this one was able to teach a quality of love, of compassion to the children of the wealthier class of people who would eventually be the leaders throughout this land area.

The second part of the reading explains the significance of the past lifetime to the present one.

We see that at the present time period that this entity does have a great deal of warmth and love that resides within this one. We do see that this one does hold the self back from offering this love, not only to others, but also to the self. We see that much of this is due to the fact that this one has continued to foster a type of fear from past hurts where this one has felt that in this one's vulnerable state, this one was misunderstood.

Would suggest to this one to seek healing in this area and practice that of forgiveness within the self and among all individuals that this one may be harboring thoughts, and emotions that are counter-productive and disharmonious to the soul.

Kathleen posed the following questions to better understand her past life reading.

The past life:
1. What were the karmic lessons?
2. What gifts, talents, and understandings were developed?
3. What was purpose of the past life?
4. How did I change and evolve during that lifetime?

Significance of the past lifetime to the present:
1. What similar thinking patterns did I carry over from the past lifetime?
2. What lessons am I facing? Are they similar to those from the past lifetime?
3. What experiences and talents developed in the past will aid me the most now?
4. What will I do differently in this lifetime?

Kathleen found several similarities between the past and the present. She recognized that the karmic lessons from her past life involved communication, an area she currently struggles with. The challenge, however, has lessened from the severe handicap of muteness to a fear of expressing her thoughts. Through courage and understanding, she has learned to express herself without fearing other people's reactions. She has also used her artistic talent to express herself through painting.

She uses teaching skills developed in the past lifetime in her position as an elementary art teacher. The reading reminded her to use her ability to teach with love and compassion, something she has been repressing. She realized this began during her childhood when she had to deal with the death of her two sisters, and later as an adult with the loss of her husband. As she showed more compassion with her students, she noticed that they were much more cooperative. She began to communicate the emotions she had been keeping inside and changed her pattern of isolation by taking classes and reaching out.

Kathleen now feels she is on the road to complete her purpose of fully communicating her thoughts and sharing her love with others. This reading gave her the motivation to overcome past hurts and sadness and fully channel her love into teaching and art.

In the next chapter we will view Kathleen's astrology chart to see how the past shaped her present.

TASKS

1. Obtain a past life profile from the School of Metaphysics in Windyville, Missouri, at 417-345-8411 or check the Web site, http://www.som.org/, for information. Past life readings may also be obtained from Bruce and Connie Compton, at 417-345-2472, or check the Web site, http:// www.celestialawakenings.com.

2. Have a past life regression session. Record the session and later transcribe it. The International Association for Regression Research and Therapies, Inc., at http://www.iarrt.org, is a nonprofit organization "dedicated to increasing the acceptance and use of professional and responsible past life therapy through education, association and research."

QUESTIONS

1. What wisdom did you gain in past lives?
2. What patterns are you repeating during this lifetime?
3. What is your karma in this lifetime?
4. What is your purpose in this lifetime?
5. How are your past and present lives similar?
6. To what extent did you fulfill your purpose in a past lifetime?

EXERCISES

1. Make a list of all resources and opportunities available to you in your current life. How can these help you evolve?
2. How do these opportunities compare to those revealed in past lives?
3. Draw a time line of the important choices you have made in this lifetime. Write down the effects of these choices.
4. Write the reasons you chose the time and country in which you were born.
5. Explain why you incarnated as a male or female.
6. Write an obituary according to how you would like to be remembered in this lifetime.
7. Draw or paint important events or a self-portrait from a past life. Display your artwork as a reminder of your soul's journey.

8. Visit countries or cultures that intrigue you and see what memories they evoke.

9. Throw a past life party. Invite your guests to dress up as they did in a past life and act out their past life behavior.

Three

Astrology:
The Stars Lead the Way

Right on Track

Jim loved his 30 years of teaching and coaching sports for youths from 15 to 22 years old. He was known for his charisma, his optimism, and his caring attitude. After several years of coaching high school track and field, he accepted the position of track and field director at San Diego State University. His new job involved more paperwork and less time with students, stresses that led him to consider changing careers.

Although Jim was fairly content with his life, he wanted to focus more on spirituality and learn more about himself. As we studied his astrology report, he realized that his many wonderful qualities qualified him for the work he was doing. He did not need a radical makeover; he simply had to make a few adjustments to find contentment.

Jim's astrological chart validated his career path: it was a perfect avenue for his talents and skills. His sun sign is Pisces, providing him with patience and a caring attitude, which helped him relate to his students. His Leo moon urged him to reach out to people, and the sports teams welcomed his charisma and ability to gain the respect of athletes. He was comforted to know that coaching track and field was aligned with his life purpose. He recognized that he wanted to change jobs because his position involved too much administration and not enough interaction with students.

He returned to coaching at community colleges. Jim, a good communicator, put this skill to use when he began announcing at events.

What was still missing was the spiritual component. He was confronted with the Pisces obstacle of putting too much attention on physical goals without enough attention on his spirituality. He saw the need to develop the natural ability of the Pisces influence to be introspective. He decided to work part-time, leaving more time for spiritual study, including past life work, meditation, and reading. He joined a church and spent time doing missionary work in Mexico. Through self-analysis and charity work, Jim grew to appreciate himself more and more.

Jim continues to devote himself to teaching and coaching sports, feeling that he's "right on track."

Astrology is a precise tool that guides us towards self-awareness. It is based on the principal "As above, so below." Planetary patterns correspond to and reflect cycles and patterns on Earth. Souls choose their time of birth to correspond to favorable planetary influences that will help them learn lessons and fulfill their karmic destiny. The planetary configurations at the time of birth imprint certain personality traits on us. The better we understand these influences, the more aware we are of our life purpose.

Most people are familiar with their Sun sign (the sign of the zodiac occupied by the Sun). Although it is the most significant part of the horoscope (a representational map of the sky, based on a particular date, time, and place of birth), it is only a portion of it. There are many other facets we must consider to get a clear picture of our astrological influences. This concept is the foundation of this book: to know oneself totally we must look at various methods of self-analysis to get the broadest picture possible. Astrology illustrates the concept that every facet of our natal chart reveals a part of the bigger picture of who we are.

Astrology teaches us that everything is connected, for example, the placement of one planet may affect another. The influence of a planet in our chart causes us to act and express ourselves in diverse ways in our environment and with the people around us.

We are motivated by physical, mental, emotional, and spiritual needs. Astrology helps us understand our needs through the study of the planets. Each planet represents a different need, drive, or desire. Throughout much of our life we seek to understand and fulfill these needs. For example, we may have a need to understand service, or a need to learn how to openly express ourselves and communicate. It is when we listen to our inner urges and act on them that we align ourselves with our life purpose.

A natal chart maps the soul's potential for a lifetime. It is not a system of categorizing people; rather, it is a map of potential, of who a person can become, revealing strengths, weaknesses, talents, abilities, and challenges. The individual chooses how to use the influences of the horoscope. By becoming aware of these influences you become more conscious of your soul's choices, gifts, and talents.

THE PLANETS

The planets include Mercury, Venus, Mars, Jupiter, Saturn, Uranus, Neptune, and Pluto. We often include the Sun and the Moon in this category, even though they are not planets. Each planet represents and reveals a drive or a need within us and describes the quality of energy every person uses.

Each planet has its own purpose. Our challenge is to express that purpose in the unique way specified by its placement in our chart. The purpose will differ for each individual, depending on the zodiacal sign and house it resides in.

Sun

The Sun represents how we want to be recognized, our creative urge, and how we express our creativity. The placement of the Sun is crucial to understanding our life purpose because it is the most influential planet on our chart. Purpose: understand our basic character.

Moon

The Moon represents our emotional nature, revealing how we nurture others and how we want to be nurtured. It also focuses on our domestic life, how we behave within a family, and how we relate to a nurturing person growing up (usually our mother). It represents our urge for security and reveals how we create a "nest" for ourselves. The Moon also reveals our feelings and sensitivities. Purpose: understand our feelings and emotions.

Mercury

Mercury is the Roman god of commerce, eloquence, travel, cunning, and theft who served as messenger to the other gods.[1] The planet Mercury relates to the mind, revealing the way we think and communicate. Depending on what sign of the zodiac Mercury is in (i.e., what sign influences Mercury, determined by planetary alignment), this planet reveals what we focus our mental abilities on, be it wealth, service, or other avenues, as well as what piques our curiosity. Purpose: communicate and develop our mental abilities.

Venus

Venus, a feminine, receptive planet, is named after the Roman goddess of love and beauty, so it reflects what we value and what we regard as beautiful. This planet reveals our sensual nature and what we see as pleasurable and joyful. It shows how we behave in intimate relationships and how we express love and affection. Venus governs marriage, appreciation, and our social natures. Purpose: learn to receive love and understand the essence of harmony.

Mars

Mars is the aggressive, male counterpart of Venus. (In Roman mythology, Mars was the god of war.) Mars represents how we initiate and take action and how we assert ourselves. Therefore, when we repress this Mars quality we often become ill. We must work with the Mars energy to promote healthy self-expression. In love, Mars represents our sexual drive. It also represents the areas in which—and how—we will be ambitious. Purpose: understand how to direct energy to manifest our desires.

Jupiter

Jupiter is the chief Roman god, the god of light, of the sky and weather, and of the state, its welfare, and its law. This planet deals with expansion, travel, luck, and opportunities. It reveals the avenues through which we receive monetary benefits and rewards from good deeds done in the past. It shows how we share our talents and generosity with others. Jupiter reveals the areas in which our optimism shines and where we hold hope and high aspirations. Purpose: learn to cause prosperity, abundance, and expansion in all areas of life.

Saturn

In Roman mythology, Saturn is the god of agriculture. Saturn is the planet of maturity and responsibility. Therefore, the sign in which it appears indicates the particular areas we need to develop. Saturn continually brings us lessons in these areas and is a strong driving force in our karma, helping us to see the cause and effect of our actions. Saturn is where we experience many challenges and limitations until we master the Saturn lessons. It indicates what types of work and responsibilities we take on and how we handle those responsibilities. Since Saturn represents what we lack, we may feel very insecure in this area. Purpose: learn responsibility, discipline, and respect structure.

The three planets that follow are the "outer" or "generational" planets. They can affect an entire generation due to their slow movement through the signs, which may account for similarities in thought among generations. These planets do not affect us as much on a personal level as do the previous seven inner planets. As Saturn provides a constant stimulus to mature in a certain area, Uranus, Neptune, and Pluto provide a constant stimulus to go beyond the ordinary and reach for transcendence. The energies of these planets can lead us down the dark road of escapism, rebelliousness, and radical negative behaviors, or towards new, more positive ways of being, thinking, and expressing ourselves. The entire consciousness of a generation can change when we harness the energy of these planets.

Uranus

In Greek mythology, Uranus is the sky personified as a god and father of the Titans, a family of giants. This planet brings us the energies of independence, change, and uniqueness. To make the best use of these energies—which can come upon us quite suddenly—we must listen to our intuition so that we are open to the flashes of insight that Uranus brings. The Uranus energy is often experienced as a desire for freedom and a desire to be different. Thus, we need to move forward and experiment with our ideas. The sign Uranus is in reveals the nature of the experimentation. When people attune themselves to the vibration of Uranus, they can use these new ideas and innovative thoughts to change old ways of being and thinking. Purpose: learn to cause change by using intuition.

Neptune

Neptune is the Roman god of the sea. Its purpose is for us to connect with our soul and the spiritual world. Neptune ignites our awareness of other worlds and higher states of consciousness. It is often associated with the part of us that wants to be swept away, or to see only the rosy part of life rather than reality. Neptune shows how we are inspired to transcend the physical, perhaps through art or religion, or by escaping with drugs or alcohol. Neptune reveals where we lack clear perception and where we place our faith. This planet rules illusions, delusion, and spirituality. It reveals how we deceive others and ourselves. We may have to sacrifice attachment to find the "ultimate" here on Earth, and realize it is only through higher spiritual ideals that the energies of Neptune can help us move toward ultimate fulfillment. Purpose: transcend the mundane physical world and reach for higher states of awareness.

A generation can use this energy toward manifesting a spiritual ideal. Neptune in Aries (1861–1875) led to the Homestead Act, the first women's suffrage law in Wyoming, and the Civil War. Neptune in Pisces (1847–1861) led to the description of a better world in *The Communist Manifesto*.

Pluto

Another Greek god is Pluto, the god of the underworld. Pluto is the planet of regeneration and transformation: death and rebirth. It brings to the forefront desires from the past that must be elevated. We can transform ourselves using Pluto's drive to delve into understanding others and ourselves at the core level. We can use the concentrated Plutonian power to advance (positive energies such as honesty and love) or to regress (negative energies such as deception and cruelty). Focusing on our spiritual nature moves us beyond the pairs of opposites to find balance and understanding. We can use Pluto's power to wipe out the old, much of which is karma from past lives, and bring in the new, which will open doors to new ways of being and to tremendous growth for future generations. Purpose: transform lower energies and emotions into a higher vibration.

Many transforming historical events illustrate the effect of this planet. When Pluto was in Aquarius (1778–1798), the United States Constitution was written, the French began their revolution, and the U.S. won independence from the British. The earth influence of Pluto in Taurus (1851–1883) gave us the U.S. transcontinental railroad and the growth of corporate America.

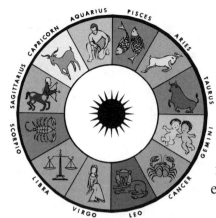

THE ZODIAC

The zodiac comprises a particular group of constellations appearing as a circle in the sky. The 360 degrees of the circle are divided into 12 sections, each occupying 30 degrees. The 12 sections correspond to the 12 signs (fields of action) and houses (fields of activity) of the zodiac. The signs are filters for the planets, influencing how a planet or house expresses its qualities.

A horoscope shows the placement of the planets among the 12 signs and the 12 houses. With a large number of possible house-sign combinations, it's unusual for any two people to have the same horoscope. Every planet, as well as the Sun and the Moon, occupies one of the 12 zodiac signs and one of the houses, depending on a person's date and time of birth.

The most significant position on an astrology chart is the Sun. Whatever sign it occupies is known as the Sun sign; it has the greatest overall effect on a person's personality. The Sun sign is based on the day of birth. Each sign is ruled by a particular planet. Therefore, gaining an understanding of the ruling planet gives greater insight into the meaning of the sign. For example, Capricorn is ruled by the planet Saturn. Saturn is the planet of responsibility and duty, so we can understand where the drive to succeed and be responsible comes from in people with Capricorn in their chart. Taurus is ruled by the planet Venus. Venus is the planet of love and beauty. Knowing this, we can see why people with Taurus in their chart enjoy material comforts and the sensual pleasures.

ELEMENTS: FIRE, EARTH, AIR, AND WATER

Each sign of the zodiac has certain strengths and gifts as well as challenges and weaknesses. With awareness and willpower we can harness the most positive qualities of each sign. The 12 zodiac signs are classified into groups describing temperament according to elements: fire, earth, air, and water.

These elements are key factors in understanding a natal chart because they reveal how we use and interpret energies. They have psychological, spiritual, and physical significance. They also reveal our life purpose by delineating our gifts, talents, and karmic lessons. The element of the Sun sign is the most significant factor, followed by the Moon and ascendant.

	Fire Signs (Aries, Leo, Sagittarius)	Earth Signs (Taurus, Virgo, Capricorn)	Air Signs (Gemini, Libra, Aquarius)	Water Signs (Cancer, Scorpio, Pisces)
Purpose	cause action, movement, and change	create and add infrastructure and objects to enhance the world	connect people, places, and things through ideas and thoughts	cause healing and greater understanding among people through the emotions
Gifts and Talents	motivating, energetic, honest, willful, enthusiastic, humorous, joyful, intense	competent, stable, practical, resourceful, creative, supportive, skilled in the sense of touch	logical, objective, social, curious, good planners, perceptive, communicative, quick intellect	sensitive, psychic, compassionate, serene, adaptable, empathetic
Karmic Lessons	patience, love, receptivity, sensitivity, stability, self-control	service, flexibility, initiative	stability, attention, sensitivity to others, express emotion and intimacy	logic, practicality, security, stability, communication

The signs of the zodiac can also be grouped into one of three qualities that illustrate the movement of energy in the physical world: cardinal, fixed, and mutable. We first initiate action, the role of cardinal signs. Next, we follow through and sustain the action, the role of the fixed signs. Finally, we complete the transformation and surrender, the role of the mutable signs.

Aries, Cancer, Libra, and Capricorn are considered cardinal or angular signs. The main influences of cardinal signs are those of initiation, ambition, independence, and activity. Each of these signs marks the change of a season: Aries: spring; Cancer: summer; Libra: fall; Capricorn: winter. These signs also relate to four life areas: Aries: personal identity; Cancer: home life; Libra: partnerships; Capricorn: career. The purpose of the cardinal quality is to initiate. The lesson is to avoid being impulsive and domineering.

Taurus, Leo, Scorpio, and Aquarius are the fixed or succedent signs. People born under these signs could make good leaders because they are stable, determined, resolute, and unwavering. They are determined and have a strong and enduring will. The purpose of the fixed quality is to cause stability. The lesson is to avoid becoming stubborn and egocentric.

Gemini, Virgo, Sagittarius, and Pisces are the mutable or common signs. Those born with these signs can be flexible, multitalented, adaptable, intuitive, versatile, and have good mental focus. The purpose of the mutable quality is to be cooperative and flexible. The lesson is to focus and avoid scattering energy in too many different directions.

SIGNS OF THE ZODIAC

A person born on a date associated with a particular sign occupied by the Sun is considered to be born "under" that Sun sign and is subject to that sign's influences. The influence of our Sun sign helps us fulfill our life purpose by providing us with certain gifts and talents. Each zodiacal signs adds to our lessons. The following descriptions list the ruler (the planet with the strongest influence) for each sign of the zodiac; the quality (mode of operating in life); and the element (temperament). The phrase in quotation marks illustrates the essence of how people under that sign express their energy. Each description closes with the lesson for each sign, a helpful gift, and an obstacle.

Aries (Ram), March 21–April 20 *(Mars, Cardinal, Fire)* "I Am"

Persons born under the sign of Aries are brave pioneers who like to be first. They have a competitive spirit and make good leaders because they know how to use their aggressive energy and initiate activity. They are driven to succeed and prove who they are. They need to be aware of tendencies to be impulsive, impatient, and pushy. Arians would benefit by including, rather than excluding, people so they can share their buoyant enthusiasm for life with others. Lesson: understand individuality. Gift: honesty and forthrightness. Obstacle: selfishness.

Taurus (Bull), April 21–May 20 *(Venus, Fixed, Earth)* "I Have"

Taurus is a practical and stable sign. Those who bear the sign of Taurus place much importance on security. In their striving for security they focus on accumulating money and possessions and may even become possessive of their partners. They can call upon their practicality to manifest their ideas in the physical world. They are here to learn about their own self-worth. They would do well to avoid placing their value outside of themselves, that is, based on what they can produce, or on their net worth, and realize that their value comes from who they are. The Venus influence heightens

27

their appreciation of beauty and the sensual pleasures in life, such as food, sex, and touch. They can overcome tendencies to be stubborn, possessive, materialistic, and argumentative by bringing out their positive qualities of patience, stability, practicality, and loyalty. Lesson: understand stability and self-worth. Gift: perseverance and persistence. Obstacle: selfishness, which restrains them from giving. Giving and receiving help people build self-worth.

Gemini (Twins), May 21–June 21 *(Mercury, Mutable, Air)* **"I Think"**

Those under the influence of this air sign experience life through the mind and spend much time fulfilling their curiosity through intellectual pursuits. With Mercury as their ruler, they are interested in all forms of communication and may choose a profession in which they can use these skills. They have many opportunities available to them due to their multitalented nature. It is important that these individuals undertake some education and training to satisfy their curious and active minds and to aid them in developing their talents. They are witty and social, attracting many friends. They can overcome tendencies to be restless and scattered by developing concentration and focus so their sharp mind can serve them well. Lesson: communicate with both inner (subconscious) and outer (conscious) minds. Gift: perception. Obstacle: a tendency to be imbalanced in communication, with too much emphasis on the conscious mind and physical things, or on the subconscious mind and spiritual things.

Cancer (Crab), June 22–July 22 *(Moon, Cardinal, Water)* **"I Feel"**

Cancers are warm, affectionate, loving, nurturing individuals. They often channel this energy into their family life, making them devoted and loyal parents who strive to protect their loved ones. Security is important to them in family and financial matters, which may lead them to be overbearing and possessive of loved ones. They prefer to carefully invest money rather than jump into risky plans, and are cautious in their personal relationships. Ruled by the Moon, they experience life through the emotions. To protect themselves from being hurt they often withdraw into a shell, symbolized by the crab. It would behoove

Cancers to express their emotions so that both they and others can reach a deeper understanding of them, and their all-encompassing love can shine. Lesson: achieve greater receptivity and balance independence and intimacy with oneself and with others. Gift: sensitivity. Obstacle: codependency and the inability to distinguish between independence and dependence.

Leo (Lion), July 23–August 22 *(Sun, Fixed, Fire)* **"I Will"**

Leo is dramatic and courageous like the symbol of the lion. These charismatic individuals are born leaders who enjoy the limelight. Ruled by the Sun, Leos are here to express themselves creatively to the world, often channeling this creativity into a career in the performing arts, or other public avenue. Leos are generous and freely give of their time, talents, and physical resources. Leo is a fixed sign and, therefore, often has difficulty yielding or giving in to others. To overcome egocentrism, Leos would do well to channel their self-confidence and high regard for self into creative self-expression or assume a position of authority, aiding others with their joyous spirit. Lesson: use energy and power with wisdom, especially with regard to leadership. Gift: generosity and an ability to forgive. Obstacle: self-centeredness.

Virgo (Virgin), August 23–September 22 *(Mercury, Mutable, Earth)* **"I Analyze"**

These practical and industrious folks usually make work and service the focal point of their lives. Ruled by Mercury, they possess a good intellect and, with practice, can develop the fine art of discrimination. They are meticulous and conscientious workers who do well in the healing professions or in jobs that require mental acumen, such as editing. Their earth influence gives them a healthy dose of sensuality and groundedness. Virgos have such a strong ability to focus that they can sometimes get caught up in trivial details and forget to see the whole picture. Their attention to detail can turn into criticalness or pickiness. Virgos can gain control over their minds by tuning into their feelings and trusting their instincts, which will help them bring forth their desires for a better world. Lesson: make wise choices for the productive good of oneself and others. Gift: ability to visualize. Obstacle: disorganization.

Libra (Balance), September 23–October 22 *(Venus, Cardinal, Air)* "I Balance"

These cooperative and sociable individuals are here to bring peace and harmony to people and to the environment. Their desire for balance gives them the ability to see things from many different viewpoints before making a decision. They often channel the desire for balance into careers that involve upholding justice, such as the legal field. They also need to satisfy their intellectual side, so they may seek mental stimulation through studies in areas such as psychology. They enjoy beauty in all forms, due to the influence of Venus. They also have a lot of focus on relationships. Marriage and companionship may be the focal point of their life. Their argumentative and indecisive behavior is their attempt at fairness so they can bring their gifts of harmony, equality, and balance to the world. Lesson: find the truth. Gift: an understanding of balance that stimulates them to search for the truth. Obstacle: fear of the truth.

Scorpio (Scorpion), October 23–November 21 *(Mars and Pluto, Fixed, Water)* "I Desire"

Scorpios are powerfully intense and passionate people who can magnetize those who come into their presence. They use their determination and will to delve into matters, often relating to the occult. They are not content to remain on the surface, so they probe, using their intuitive and perceptive minds, until they find answers. They often channel their investigative minds into upholding justice and uncovering foul play. However, when it comes to revealing themselves they can be very secretive. Yet they can't hide their strong emotions and intense passions, which makes them irresistible. They must exercise emotional control so as not to be destructively ruled by their strong emotions and passions. They have great power due to the influence of their rulers Mars and Pluto. Their challenge is to use this power wisely to cause transformation in themselves and the world. When they become vengeful (the notorious sting of the scorpion), jealous, and secretive, it is simply a misdirection of their energy which, when channeled positively, allows them to be the powerful creators they are capable of being. Lesson: express true feelings and ideas to realize their desires. Gift: an understanding of wholeness and how to build self-worth. Obstacle: the need to gain approval of others, which causes them to lose sight of their true desires.

Sagittarius (Archer), November 22–December 21 *(Jupiter, Mutable, Fire)* "I See"

These optimistic, enthusiastic, fun-loving individuals naturally attract many friends. They are good conversationalists, but others may have difficulty getting a word in edgewise. They love freedom and feel most at home out of doors and traveling the globe. You can count on Sagittarians to tell you the truth, but beware: sometimes their bluntness can be brutal. They have the gifts of broadmindedness and insight. These outgoing people have a serious side when dealing with philosophical matters, religion, and societal concerns. They search for new avenues of knowledge that may lead them to study spirituality. They must be careful that their idealism does not turn into fanaticism. Keeping a Sagittarian's attention can be a challenge because they get bored so easily. Do not limit them in any way or you will be sure to lose them quickly. They can overcome their tendencies to be impatient, argumentative, exaggerative, and procrastinators with their broadmindedness and insight. Lesson: excel in and identify with spirituality. Gift: strong perception and a high level of motivation. Obstacle: too much identification with the physical, leading them to abandon their spirituality and jump from one thing to the next.

Capricorn (Goat), December 22–January 19 *(Saturn, Cardinal, Earth)* "I Use"

The Capricorn influence produces practical, conscientious, trustworthy, and responsible individuals, some of the hardest working of all the signs of the zodiac. As earth signs, they focus to a great extent on acquiring financial security, sometimes losing sight of the importance of work over money. They may overwork themselves but are usually able to attain their goals with their strong work ethic and good organizational and managerial skills. Due to Saturn's influence, they can handle a lot of responsibility. With their methodical approach to life and ambition they can be quite successful. Lesson: learn how to cause change. Gift: productivity. Obstacle: the tendency to feel inadequate, which restrains them from initiating activity.

Aquarius (Water Bearer), January 20–February 18 *(Uranus, Fixed, Air)* "I Know"

These independent and progressive thinkers are humanitarians. They are great visionaries capable of motivating and leading groups of people towards fulfilling their futuristic ideals. Aquarians often rally behind a cause for justice. Being a fixed sign, they rarely waiver from their position and must guard against being too stubborn and dictatorial. They have a sharp, logical, and intellectual mind that they often use towards scientific or inventive pursuits. Aquarians are everyone's friend; they feel most at home in large groups of people.

One-on-one interactions are more challenging for these temperamental souls because they sometimes get too fixed on their own way of thinking and alienate others who do not share their viewpoint. They can use their vision to stimulate themselves if they fall into lazy and undisciplined behavior. Their humane and altruistic personalities shine the brightest when sharing their love with humanity. Lesson: teach humanity. Gift: leadership abilities and a love for humanity. Obstacle: uncertainty, self-doubt.

Pisces (Fishes), February 19–March 20 (Neptune and Jupiter, Mutable, Water) "I Believe"

These compassionate, intuitive beings are sensitive to other people's feelings as well as to the suffering of mankind. Their emotions often lead them in two different directions (hence, the symbol of the two fishes swimming in opposite directions). Their challenge is to gain emotional clarity by learning to separate their own thoughts from those of others. They would do well to work at gaining self-awareness to maintain their unique identity. Pisces can channel their vivid imaginations into creative endeavors such as art, dance, and music. They can overcome their tendency to live in a dream world by staying connected to humanity through the healing arts or other service-related fields where their charitable natures can shine. Lesson: the ability to look at a situation from all angles. Gift: introspection. Obstacle: too much attention on the past and on physical accomplishments and too little attention on building their own character and identity.

OPPOSITE SIGNS: LEARNING OPPORTUNITIES

Opposite signs present great learning opportunities because they embody opposite qualities. We do not experience the opposite energy as an influence directed at us, however, the zodiac signs in our chart activate the polar opposite. People with opposite signs, particularly the Sun sign, can help us fulfill our life purpose by helping us become aware of opposite qualities we may lack. By incorporating some of these opposite qualities, we can achieve a more balanced state. Often, we understand these opposite qualities to some degree but we need to explore and develop them to a greater extent. (Haven't you ever wondered why opposites attract?)

Following is a brief look at the learning opportunities offered by our opposite zodiacal influence.

Aries and Libra

Both Arians and Librans need to learn how to behave in relationships. Aries can be too independent, egocentric, and selfish to form long-lasting unions. Libra often tries too hard to blend in with the crowd and harmonize to be liked by everyone. Each can achieve balance by integrating both of these qualities. Aries can learn to be more cooperative and put others' needs first, and Librans can learn to express their individuality, even in a relationship, so they don't lose themselves in another person or group. In essence, one needs self-awareness to be able to form deep and meaningful unions with others.

Aries must remember that a great deal of self-awareness can be gained in relationships with other people. You cannot be a leader and exclude the needs of others, nor can you always blend in with others and never take your own stand on issues. To be effective you need a combination of both. Aries can learn how to love others from Libra, and Libra can learn to love himself more by spending time alone and in pursuits dedicated to self-awareness. Aries can learn to be less impulsive and consider various viewpoints before making decisions. Libra can learn to be more decisive and less wishy-washy. Relationships can be rewarding for both of these influences when Libra relinquishes his tendency toward dependence and compromising, and forms a relationship that fosters independence and uniqueness. Aries can learn from

Libra how to cooperate and reach others through love and harmony, rather than through force and aggression.

Taurus and Scorpio

These individuals are here to balance material and spiritual needs and values. The tendency of Taureans is to place too much emphasis on materiality, measuring their self-worth based on monetary worth and the ability to acquire physical possessions. Scorpions, on the other hand, focus their energy on spiritual pursuits, often to the extent of renouncing the physical world altogether. Taurus can learn to let go of attachments to the physical world and transcend his interests into the spiritual realm (Scorpio). Scorpio can learn from Taurus how to function in the physical world. Both need to learn how to be "in the world but not of it."

Taurus and Scorpio both have the ability to create. Taureans often create just for the sake of creating, so they need to use their creativity for spiritual purposes and to serve the Creator. Taurus has a keen sense of power over the physical world, while Scorpio wields power over the occult and all that governs the underworld. Both need to wield their power productively. Scorpio needs to use power to attain higher states of consciousness, while at the same time not shutting out the physical. Taureans can use their determination and self-discipline to remain dedicated to a spiritual path.

Gemini and Sagittarius

These individuals are here to learn about the mind and about communication. Gemini understands things from an intellectual standpoint and uses logic and reasoning to reach understanding. Sagittarians learn from listening to their intuition and wisdom, which comes from revelations they receive from the higher self. These signs can find balance by using logic to understand the insights that come from the higher self, and then applying them in the physical world. If we work just with facts (Gemini), we remain at a physical level only, so Gemini can learn from Sagittarius how to go beyond facts and embrace intuitive insights. Sagittarians need to apply their philosophical ideas to the physical world through reasoning and logic (Gemini). When there is a balance between ideals and logic, communication flows easily for these individuals and they can be effective as teachers, lecturers, and writers.

Cancer and Capricorn

Cancers can help Capricorns be more flexible and sensitive. Capricorns can help Cancers to be more ambitious and use their energies toward some work endeavor. Internally, both need to balance the masculine and feminine energies, so they are neither too watery and sensitive (Cancer), nor too cold, driven, and ambitious (Capricorn). Capricorns may have difficulty expressing their emotions and need to learn from Cancers more about emotional expression. Cancers devote their energies to the home and family, while Capricorns devotes their energy to the workplace. Both need to achieve balance among the home, family, work, and career. Until then, they may experience inner turmoil around these issues.

Leo and Aquarius

Leos and Aquarians are here to learn the art of self-expression and how to love. Leo is a fire sign that enthusiastically and generously spreads love to friends, family, and the self. Leos bring intense passion to their love relationships. Aquarians express love most easily in large groups, resulting from the urge to serve humanity at large. They have some difficulty on a one-on-one basis and can learn from Leo how to be less impersonal. Leos sometimes can be egocentric and can learn from Aquarians how to expand their vision to include more people. Aquarians are so devoted to group causes that they can lose themselves in the group; they can learn from Leo how to give themselves credit and acknowledge their efforts. Leos can learn from their opposite sign how to let go of egotism and self-centeredness, serve humanity, and sacrifice personal ambitions to aid the world.

Virgo and Pisces

Virgo is a detail-oriented organizer who separates the whole into parts for greater understanding. However, they often get lost in the details and lose sight of the bigger picture. Pisces focuses more on the whole and is a great visionary, seeing how all the pieces fit together. The downfall of Pisceans is forgetting important details and losing themselves in the grand picture. Both can be more effective by recognizing the need for understanding details to see how they fit into the whole. Virgos can get so caught up in achieving goals that they forget the vision. They can be too practical, narrow, and pessimistic in their thinking. Pisces can be too dreamy, getting lost in fantasies. There is a need for both to be practical and have focus, while still using their imagination to keep the vision alive. Virgo's overly analytical mind can block the intuition that flows easily through Pisces. Virgo can use discipline and purity of mind to reach higher states of bliss, while Pisces can use perception to tap into these higher realms. Pisceans can learn from Virgos how to be more realistic and practical, how to bring dreamy visions into reality, how to use keen discrimination, and how to discern their own thoughts from those of others. Virgos would do well to accept themselves and others more, and to learn compassion (Pisces).

THE 12 HOUSES OF THE ZODIAC

Houses are divisions of space based on Earth's 24-hour rotation. Houses describe how the influences enter into a person's life and how the planets and zodiacal signs influence the individual. Each house is influenced by a particular zodiac sign as well as the planet or planets which rule the sign. The houses have no life of their own. Rather, the house creates the stage on which a particular sign will express itself. For example, if Gemini is in the seventh house of partnership and marriage, we will express and learn about communication through our partnerships with others (marriage, friendships, and business associations).

Houses indicate the areas in which our karmic lessons will play out. If we have several planets in a particular house, many of our experiences will be focused in that area—be it service, communication, or partnerships. If someone has no planets in a house, then it means it is not a strong influence that the person wanted or needed in life.

Houses one through six relate to the self. Each one builds upon the next, so that as we progress through each house we develop qualities that help us move to the next house or area of life. The progression through the houses allows us to add understandings in many different areas:

1. We establish our self-identity.
2. Once we know ourselves we can accumulate resources.
3. We develop mind capabilities to use our resources.
4. With a developed mind and plenty of resources we are now ready to establish a foundation that will become our home.
5. With a secure home foundation we can focus on the development of our creativity.
6. We have built enough within ourselves to share our wisdom and time with the world through some form of service.

The following descriptions list the sign and planetary rulers for each house.

First House (Aries; Mars)

The first house has the qualities of Aries, which are initiative, new beginnings, self-expression, courage, and action. This house is about identity, revealing personality and expression. It reveals our approach to life and how we see the world.

The cusp (a line that separates one house from the next) of the first house is called the "ascendant."

Second House (Taurus; Venus)

This is the house of comfort and security. It deals with the acquisition of physical resources, financial matters, and how we establish security. It also reveals how we gauge our self-worth and value.

Third House (Gemini; Mercury)

This is the house of communication and the mind. It deals with the processing and assimilation of information, perception, and logic. Since an air sign resides here, there is a heavy focus on the workings of the mind, particularly on the discrimination process. It carries the Gemini qualities of curiosity, adaptability, and versatility.

Fourth House (Cancer; Moon)

This house is concerned with security and the home. It reveals information about the nature of the home and the family we grew up with, as well as the type of dwelling we will create for ourselves when we mature. It reveals our roots, and how we use our nurturing and protective qualities.

Fifth House (Leo; Sun)

This is the house of creativity. The Leo qualities of self-expression and love are channeled through this house. Activities related to travel, adventure, love affairs, children, teaching, and the performing arts are emphasized in this house. It shows how we express joy and vitality.

Sixth House (Virgo; Mercury)

This house is the house of duty, concerned with attitudes towards work, service, and health/hygiene-related issues. How we view work and the type of work we choose is shown here. Since it is ruled by Mercury, this house deals with mental analysis and discrimination.

Houses seven through 12 show how we relate to other people and interact with individuals and groups. It shows how we express tendencies of the opposite house with other individuals. For example, the seventh house is opposite the first house, the eighth house is opposite the second house, and so on. If the first house reveals how we express our individuality, then the seventh house shows how we harmonize and relate to others.

Seventh House (Libra; Venus)

This is the partnership house dealing with unions of all kinds, such as marriage, friendships, and business partnerships. Its ruler, Venus, brings out what we value as beautiful and our ideas about love. This house reveals the nature of the mates we attract and our ideas about marriage. Saturn is exalted, or expressed harmoniously, in this house, so the unfoldment of karma will play an important role here. This house is about Libra's quest for cooperation and balance.

Eighth House (Scorpio; Mars and Pluto)

This is the opposite of the second house, so it deals with how we handle financial resources with family and partners. It concerns money matters including wills, taxes, inheritances, trusts, and money accumulated in partnerships and business ventures. Due to the influence of Scorpio and Pluto, there is an interest in the occult, death, regeneration, and transformation.

Ninth House (Sagittarius; Jupiter)

In contrast to what one personally thinks, as revealed in the third house, the ninth house shows the thinking of a collective group consciousness reflected in philosophy, religion, legal systems, science, psychology, and teachings of higher education. The expansion and inspiration from Jupiter and Neptune help us tap into a collective consciousness to see the needs of society. Travel is also associated with this house.

Tenth House (Capricorn; Saturn)

This house deals with how we use our ambitions and into what professional/career arena we channel these ambitions. It reveals our responsibilities to the world and the reputation we build for ourselves. It reveals how we respond to law, government, and other business systems.

Eleventh House (Aquarius; Uranus and Saturn)

This house is about social consciousness. It shows how we express our creativity within a group, as opposed to the individual creativity expressed in the opposite fifth house. It focuses on how we relate to people outside of intimate relationships. The influence of Aquarius here is interested in humanitarian concerns on a large scale and how groups of people work together to achieve some ideal that will minister to humanity at large.

Twelfth House (Pisces; Neptune and Jupiter)

The twelfth house uncovers hidden thoughts and behaviors. It reveals patterns and habits. It also reveals our karma. Therefore, it stores what we try to hide, those unconscious drives we are not even aware of. To work with this house we must face both karma and unconscious behaviors. It deals with the psychological and physical health of a culture, and is, therefore, concerned with group health organizations such as mental institutions, ashrams, and hospitals. The influence of Neptune here can cause us to deceive ourselves or cloud our perception of reality. There is also the possibility of developing artistic talents and compassion for those less fortunate by drawing on the Piscean energy that occupies this house.

INTERPRETING THE HOROSCOPE

With this understanding of the main elements of astrology, we can now obtain and interpret our own natal chart, a map illustrating the heavens at the time and place of birth. The horoscope shows the placement of the Sun, the Moon, the ascendant, and the planets. There are three ways to obtain a natal chart:

1. Consult an astrologer. To ensure an accurate reading, look for a certified astrologer. There are several organizations that provide references for certified astrologers who are available for consultation by the general public. Two such organizations are the American Federation of Astrologers and the NCGR. Contact information for both is listed in the resource section at the back of the book.
2. Buy astrological software. After you enter your complete name, birth date, city, state or country, and time of birth, the computer will generate a natal chart.
3. Consult an ephemeris, available in book form. This lists the planetary positions for each day as well as the sign each planet was in and the position or degree of each planet.

COMBINING THE INFLUENCES

The art of interpreting a chart involves combining information about the planet, the zodiacal sign it is in, and its house position to form a coherent message. For example, Mercury residing in Libra indicates that one's communication style focuses on achieving fairness, cooperation, and balance. Logical career choices include arbitration and diplomacy. Mercury in the ninth house shows a preference for communicating about philosophical ideas or spirituality. With a broad, expansive mind, such a person would make a good student and teacher.

The next step is to combine the information into various life areas. I have outlined five areas that should be considered in a chart reading.

Personality

We begin our chart interpretation by getting a basic understanding of our personality, character, and identity. The most important aspects of personality to investigate include:
1. The Sun.
2. The Moon.
3. The Ascendant, or rising sign, which is on the cusp of the first house. The cusp separates one house from another. The zodiacal sign on the cusp influences the energy of the house. The rising sign represents how we appear to the world, how people perceive us, and our approach to life. It shows what needs to be the focus in our mind, and the learning or quality that needs to be a part of our consciousness.
4. The first house.

Home and Family

A study of these areas on our chart shows us why we chose our parents.
1. The IC (immune coeli) is the cusp of the fourth house. This describes how an individual will experience and deal with home and family issues.
2. The fourth house.
3. The Sun represents our father and offers information about our relationship with him.
4. The Moon represents our mother and reveals how we relate to her and the nurturing quality in ourselves.
5. The third house holds information about our siblings and relatives.

Relationships

Many of our karmic lessons will be stimulated by our interactions with others.
1. The planets of love, Mars and Venus, reveal how you use your feminine and masculine energies. Mars and Venus both in air signs indicates that you would approach love from an intellectual standpoint; mental stimulation will be important for you in relationships. If these planets reside in earth signs, you will have a sensual streak and enjoy earthy pleasures. The areas where you will most likely express love and beauty depend on the houses in which these planets reside. For example, if your Venus is in the third house, you will derive pleasure from anything involving the mind and communication. You will express beauty through some form of communication (writing, singing, etc.).

2. The Moon motivates you to find a long-term mate and reveals your vulnerable nature. A Gemini Moon indicates that you will nurture others with your intellect.

3. The Descendant, the sign on the cusp of the seventh house, describes your learning in relationships. If Capricorn is on the cusp, you will approach love with caution. However, once committed, you will remain a loyal companion who is willing to work at keeping the relationship strong.

4. The fifth house reveals more of your romantic style and how you approach dating.

5. The eleventh house describes your behavior in friendships.

Career and Education

Many of us fulfill a large portion of our life purpose through a job. By studying these planets and houses you can learn which career would best help you fulfill your life purpose.

1. Saturn will urge us toward certain careers that will stimulate our deficient areas of learning.

2. Mercury.

3. Once again the Sun is included in the career portion of the interpretation: it indicates where we want to shine and make our claim to fame.

4. The MC (midheaven), located on the cusp of the tenth house, represents a talent or understanding that can be used to advance a career path.

5. The tenth house.

6. The sixth house.

7. The second house.

8. The third house.

9. The fifth house.

Spirituality

We are a spirit having a physical experience. Therefore, a life purpose always includes our spiritual development. The following planets and houses relate to our spirituality:

1. The planet Neptune.

2. The planet Pluto.

3. The planet Uranus.

4. The eighth house.

5. The ninth house.

6. The twelfth house.

KARMA

Astrology is a valuable tool for understanding our karma. The natal chart is a representation of our karma and our future. Awareness of our astrological influences can inspire us to actively pursue learning our karmic lessons.

There are specific elements of a natal chart that merit special attention as excellent karmic indicators. The first of these is the planet Saturn whose purpose is to help us mature and become responsible in areas in which we lack awareness. It continually gives us that "kick in the butt" until we mature and gain the needed awarenesses. It is the area in a chart where the individual experiences the most challenges, frustrations, and limitations, where our energy is blocked, stifling our creativity.

To know our karmic lessons, we need to see what sign Saturn is in. Suppose Saturn were in Aries. Aries deals with identity, self-assertion, and initiative. So, those with Saturn in Aries need to learn about who they are and how to assert themselves. They may find themselves in situations where they need to stand up for what they believe and speak their truth or risk being dominated by others. Refer to the list of zodiacal signs to see Saturn's lessons when it resides in the other 11 signs.

The twelfth house is known as the "karmic house" because it contains much of what we have avoided in the past. It reveals many of our unconscious drives and motives. This house reveals lessons that still need to be understood.

RETROGRADE PLANETS

Retrograde planets appear to be moving backward. This occurs when the Earth passes an outer planet that is moving more slowly or when an inner planet passes the Earth. Retrograde planets show areas where we tend to slide, requiring strong self-discipline to counteract those areas. If ignored, such areas can cause imbalance in the rest of the chart.

ASPECTS

Another element of astrology indicating important karma is the aspects (the angular measurement between two planets) of the chart. Harmonious aspects (those measuring 0, 60, or 120 degrees) show us our gifts and talents. Challenging aspects reveal areas where we will experience difficulty and tension. These are areas we have not fully developed and, therefore, are lessons we need to learn. Some of the most important aspects are conjunction (unifying and blending); sextile (harmony and compatibility); square (conflict or competition and challenges); trine (harmony and natural talents); and opposition (two opposing factors which can be harmonized by incorporating into yourself a balance between the two opposing polarities.) Other aspects of a lesser impact include the inconjunct or quincunx (difficult to combine, different desires, incompatibility); semi-sextile (an easy aspect that can lead to growth); semisquare (a minor problem which causes friction or irritation); sesquisquare (a minor problem which causes agitation).

The most significant challenging aspects are squares (90 degrees) and oppositions (180 degrees). Contrary to what many people believe, these challenging aspects are not always bad. In fact, due to the tension they provoke within a person, they offer the most opportunity for growth. The conflict acts as a stimulus to reach a resolution. It is during this process that tremendous growth can occur. The degree of transformation that can be achieved equals the amount of effort the individual puts into it.

Square

A square aspect represents a challenge. When understood it can be a major step forward in growth—a turning point. The planets that square each other have different purposes and, therefore, interfere with each other's expression. The challenge here is to create cooperation between these two forces by understanding the two energies and, with skill, blending them into harmony. The Sun represents the personality and the Moon our emotions. So, for example, when the Sun "squares" the Moon, the result is that the head says one thing and the heart or emotions say another. We need to understand how to blend thinking and feeling. Until then we will be blocked and frustrated.

The Sun-Moon relationship also reveals how we behave in relationships and how we feel about ourselves, how we blend our emotions with our personality. In the square scenario, people have trouble connecting with their feelings; since they often do not accept their emotions, they feel disharmony within themselves. The challenge is to listen to their feelings.

Opposition

Another challenging aspect is an opposition, which indicates a polarization between two signs such as Aries (exclusiveness) and Libra (inclusiveness). The key is to be aware of and achieve a balance between the two extremes.

The harmonious aspects are those that come easily. The most significant harmonious aspects include sextiles, trines, and some conjunctions. A conjunction is neutral, however if used productively, there is potential for harmony. They reveal gifts and talents that have been developed in past lives and that are meant to be used to fulfill our life purpose.

There is not much tension involved with planets that are in harmonious aspect, so the potential for growth is not as great as with challenging aspects. Harmonious aspects reveal what we have already developed so not much effort is required to bring them out. We simply need to tap into these skills and use them.

The key to using both types of aspects successfully is to use as a foundation the gifts and talents emphasized by the harmonious aspects while you master the more challenging aspects of your chart.

Sextile

This occurs when two planets are 60 degrees (two signs) apart. This position enhances the planets' ability to compliment each other. This cooperation makes it easy to learn something new: combining the two energies creates a pathway for new opportunities. The possible sextile combinations are fire and air signs and earth and water signs.

Trine

This occurs when two planets are 120 degrees (four signs) apart. There is a harmonious flow of energy between the planets involved, indicating skills, talents, and abilities that come easily, needing little effort to tap into these abilities. Sometimes this can result in laziness as we fall into the least line of resistance. Perhaps we may not even be conscious of these abilities; they may go untapped for a lifetime, which emphasizes the importance of obtaining an astrological report. Learning this information at a young age allows us to build on them over time. A grand trine is made up of three planets in the same element (fire, earth, air, or water), each about 120 degrees apart.

Conjunction

A conjunction involves two to three planets all within an orb of seven degrees. There is an intensification of themes from the planets involved in the conjunction. The planets will usually reside in the same zodiacal sign, and intensify each other's energy. Since a conjunction intensifies the energies, it manifests a strong need or emphasis within an area of a person's life depending on the planets and the signs they are in.

MOON

The Moon is associated with karma because it represents our past. Many people feel very comfortable expressing the behaviors of the Moon sign, since this was a prominent influence in past lives. In fact, some people relate more easily to their Moon sign than to their Sun sign. Our past patterns and the most comfortable ways we express ourselves come from the Moon influence. If the chart reveals challenging aspects to the Moon, we may have a negative self-image and will not feel at ease with ourselves because that "at home" feeling built in past lives is being challenged. It's important to identify which behaviors associated with the Moon serve us and which are no longer needed.

NODES OF THE MOON

Nodes are the intersecting orbit points of the Moon and Earth. One aspect of the Moon that reveals our karma is the South Node. The sign the South Node is in shows what qualities and personality behaviors have been developed. The house the Node resides in shows in which arena/activities these behaviors usually manifest themselves.

The South Node represents all the understandings and experiences from past lives, revealing things that come easily to us. We must use the South Node productively by not dwelling in the past and comfortably remaining in old behavior modes. Rather, we must use the South Node lessons to see the effects of our actions, both positive and negative, and let go of negative patterns and whatever no longer serves your highest good. We can then use the positive qualities and add to the understandings built previously. Because South Node patterns are so ingrained in us, this behavior is sometimes unconscious and habitual.

To go beyond the limitations of the past we need to move toward the North Node. It always resides in the sign and house opposite the South Node. By embracing the opposite qualities of the North Node we overcome the limitations of the South Node. The North Node reveals the qualities and understandings we need to develop during this lifetime. Since the North Node points to the future and contains behaviors not yet encountered, it may be a challenge, at first, to work with these new factors. Some people may experience fear at stepping into what the North Node offers simply because it is new. We must embrace the curiosity that leads to this virgin territory, which encompasses the major lessons to be learned by the soul during this lifetime.

To master these lessons and fully assimilate new behaviors require awareness, diligence, patience, and courage throughout our lifelong journey.

The Nodes are like two magnets pulling us in different directions. The South Node pulls us to the old, familiar past behaviors, that is, what comes easily to us. The North Node pulls us away from the old behaviors to new territory, to areas we have not explored in past lives. It is the excitement of what lies in the unknown that is the impetus for us to leave the old familiar ground to new arenas of expression. The key to working with the polarity created by the North and South Nodes is to use the past understandings and strengths (South Node) as a foundation to move forward with awareness (knowing what sign and house your North Node resides in) and curiosity, and incorporating the lessons of this new area slowly and with compassion for the self. The person needs to balance these two qualities in order to stabilize their life.

Knowledge of the Nodes helps us fulfill our soul's purpose. Embracing North Node qualities allows us to learn karmic lessons; embracing South Node qualities brings forth gifts and talents to share with others.

KARMIC ASTROLOGY

We see that astrology charts reflect talents built in past lives as well as lessons yet to be mastered. Karmic astrology links our past lives to the present. A past life reading enables us to understand ourselves and the astrological chart we created in this lifetime. I will use Kathleen's astrology chart and compare it with the information from her past life reading outlined in Chapter 2.

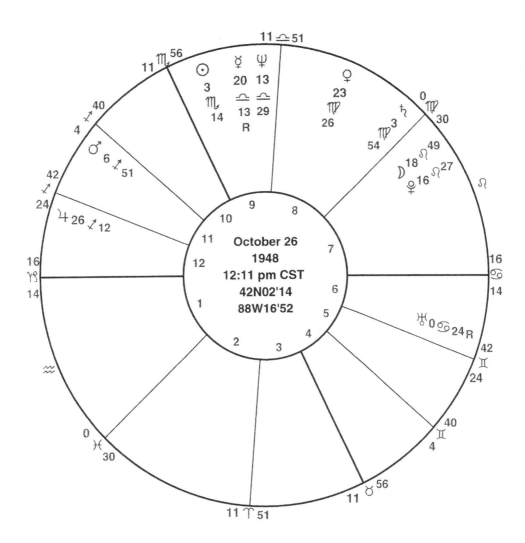

Talents gained in the past life include teaching, communication skills, compassion, and generosity. Talents seen on the astrology chart:

1. Her teaching skills are present in the heavy concentration of planets in her ninth house.

2. Her communication skills are present in the placement of Mercury in Libra, indicating an ability to write or express with beauty and harmony. Its location in the ninth house indicates that she wants to use her communication skills in teaching.

3. Her moon is in Leo, making it easy for her to be a compassionate, loving person.

4. Her generosity appears in the planets Jupiter, and Mars, which are both in the generous sign of Sagittarius.

LESSONS

Kathleen's lessons from the past life report include overcoming fears of being hurt, practicing forgiveness, fully expressing her love, and no longer isolating herself. Lessons seen on the astrology chart:

1. Her Sun is in the sign of Scorpio, which explains her tendency to withdraw if she fears being hurt. She can overcome this by mastering the Scorpio purpose: to express one's true thoughts and feelings. Scorpio also needs to learn forgiveness. She has Pluto in Leo, which shows that she needs to let go of old ways of loving in relationships and transform how she relates to others.

2. Her tendency to isolate herself can be overcome since all but one planet is in the Southern hemisphere, urging her to interact with other people.

With the help of her past life reading, Kathleen was better able to understand and use her astrological influences to the fullest. The following chart of a well-known figure in history is another example of how to use the full potential of astrological influences.

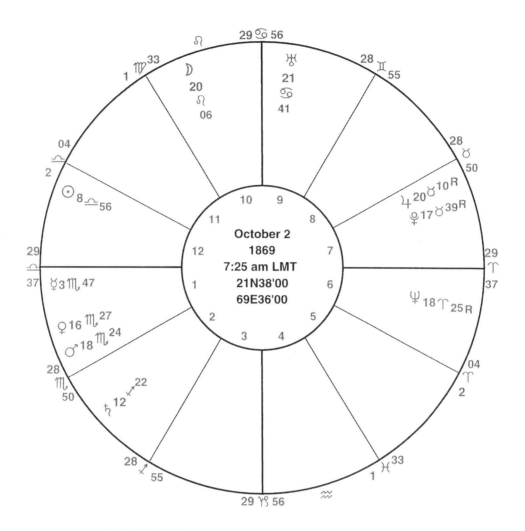

A Spiritual Statesman

Born in India on October 2, 1869, Mohandas Gandhi followed the urge of the Libra influence (Sun in Libra and Libra ascendant) to bring balance and justice to the world by attending law school in his early years. A natural diplomat, he approached his goal of freedom for India from a spiritual perspective, due to the position of his Sun in the twelfth house. Throughout his career in politics, Gandhi maintained his connection to God. His heavy Scorpio influence in Mars, Venus, and Mercury shaped his desire for a simple, austere life of selfless action. His spiritual dictionary was the Baghavad Gita, *the Indian holy text.*

Gandhi preached the need for peace and service to mankind. We can understand his sensitivity to violence through the influence of Cancer on the Midheaven. His desire for service comes from the influence of Neptune in Aries in his sixth house, which propelled him to organize the Indian Ambulance Corps for the British, and later found the Natal Indian Congress to support the rights of the Indian minority.

He utilized the power of his placement of Uranus in Cancer in the ninth house to reform religious and spiritual perspectives and revolutionize ethics and morals in India. He often challenged the status quo, which led to over 2,000 days of imprisonment. He developed steadfastness through his six planets in fixed signs. He fasted for long periods and took a vow of celibacy. He was unwavering in his support of India's cotton industry, wearing only a simple loincloth made from homespun cotton.

His nurturing disposition, combined with his warmth and charisma (Moon in Leo), helped him rise to the top of Indian politics in 1919. Thousands of people respected him as the Mahatma, the great soul, and some even considered Mohandas Gandhi the incarnation of God.

TASKS

1. Obtain a complete astrological natal chart.
2. Read a book on astrology to learn the various Sun signs and planets.
3. Find the Sun sign of each family member. Describe what you learned from each person.
4. Find the Sun signs of former partners and friends. Is there a pattern of attracting people with the same sign? If so, what do you need to learn from that influence?

QUESTIONS

1. What are the main strengths and weaknesses of your Sun sign?
2. Based on the Sun sign, what is your purpose?
3. What are your Moon and rising signs?
4. Answer questions 1 and 2 for the Moon and rising signs.
5. What are your karmic lessons based on your Moon, Saturn, South and North Nodes, twelfth house, and challenging aspects?
6. What are your lessons in love? (based on placement of Venus and Mars and fifth and seventh house activity)
7. What are your lessons regarding the emotions? (based on the placement of the Moon)
8. What is your style of communication? (based on the placement of Mercury)
9. What can you learn from your opposite Sun sign?
10. What does your chart reveal about your career potential?

EXERCISES

1. Make a collage based on your Sun, Moon, and rising signs depicting the qualities of each.
2. Choose one quality of your astrological makeup and practice it that day. For example, if your Sun sign is Virgo, practice service for one day, assisting everyone you meet.
3. Look at the list of choices you have made in this lifetime. Examine how your astrological makeup influenced your choices.

4. List the ways your astrological strengths can help you overcome your karma.

5. Write a plan of the opportunities you have to transform yourself using Neptune, Uranus, and Pluto as guidelines.

[1] Definitions of the gods' names are from *Merriam Webster's Collegiate Dictionary, Tenth Edition* (Springfield, Massachusetts: Merriam-Webster, Incorporated, 1993).

Four

Numerology: Adding It Up

$3+6+4+$
$5=9$
$L+O+V+E$
$2+0+0+3=5$

Countdown to Success

Sarah moved to Chicago the day after college graduation to begin her career in an entry-level sales and marketing position. After more than 10 years of hard work, driven to excel, she rose through the ranks to a marketing/advertising management position.

Along with her ambitious, corporate side, Sarah was intuitive and introspective. In fact, she attributed much of her business savvy to her ability to read people and foresee business opportunities. Despite her success, she felt empty and yearned to affect people on a deeper level.

Her numerology chart pointed to an extremely high potential for success. She had no karmic lessons. Her life path number 9 indicated that during this lifetime, she must complete a cycle of learning and apply the wisdom she built during the first eight cycles to serve humanity. (She always knew that she was here to do something big.) Sarah, tired of the corporate world that hindered her creativity, dreamed of opening her own business.

After completing The Artist's Way *workshop, Sarah pursued her creativity through painting, designing, and exhibiting crafts she makes at local arts shows. Sarah thought that another good way to positively influence*

*humanity would be as a professional coach. She en-
rolled in a coach certification program with plans of
starting her own practice.*

*To live up to the potential of her expression number 7,
Sarah intensely pursued spiritual study and personal
growth work. She worked through the six approaches to
self-awareness depicted in this book and continues to study
her dreams and the inner workings of her mind.*

*As Sarah develops the potential that her life path and ex-
pressions numbers offer her, she will more readily bring
out her hidden passion number 1: to be a pioneer and
leader at the forefront of change. She is on her way to
successfully combining her knowledge of the business
world with her intuitive abilities.*

Numerology is another tool we can use to access our life purpose, revealing our gifts and talents and our karma. Numerology provides us with an outline of this lifetime's potential, as well as a year-by-year synopsis of the challenges and opportunities that lie ahead.

Through the study of numerology we discover that our world is not one of chance, rather, we live in a very orderly, balanced world in which numbers play an important role. Just as your astrological makeup is not an accident, neither is your birth date or your name. Your soul chose the time and date of birth to offer itself the most appropriate lessons. Your parents intuitively chose your name to best suit you.

Numerology is an ancient system of the study of numbers. The ancient Egyptians' belief in the power of numbers was so strong that everything in their society, from weddings to planting time, to the date that they would construct temples, was based on numbers. Many cultures have developed numerology systems in an attempt to understand the universe. The method used in this book is based on the Western Pythagorean system. Pythagoras was a philosopher, astronomer, and astrologer who revealed the mystery of numbers to the world.

Numerologists have discovered that every number expresses a certain vibration, or personality. We are drawn to a certain number because of the qualities and characteristics it represents. No number is better than another; each is unique and necessary to embody the different energies that exist. Each number has both positive and negative aspects. It is up to us to determine how we will apply the gift of numbers—the numerical influences—in our life.

Numerology works predominantly with the numbers 1 through 9. Therefore, when we add a series of numbers, we reduce two-digit numbers to a single digit with (in most cases) the exception of the master numbers, 11 and 22. Each number expresses the opposite qualities of the preceding number. For example, 1 expresses the energy of independence, leadership, and individuality, while 2 represents cooperation, partnerships, and balance. The shape of the number reflects its vibration. For example, the number 8 reflects the union of the physical and spiritual, represented by the two joined circles.

The letters of the alphabet are also assigned numbers. The letter A has a value of 1, B has a value of 2, and so on until you reach 9 (I). Then begin again by assigning the number 1 to the letter J. Since each letter has a numerical value, we can use numerology to discover the meaning of names. This also explains why we are more attracted to certain words than to others. Just as your name perfectly suits you, so does every word beautifully embrace the quality of the object it describes. Think of the sound "love." Adding the numerical values of the letters in "love" (3 + 6 + 4 + 5 = 18; 1 + 8 = 9) comes out to 9, the number of the humanitarian, symbolizing unconditional love for people.

QUALITIES OF NUMBERS

The following table lists the positive and negative qualities of the numbers 1 through 9 and the master numbers 11 and 22. The master numbers have more potential than other numbers due to the powerful energy behind them.

	Positive Qualities	Negative Qualities
1	authoritative, ambitious, independent, courageous, pioneering, aggressive, dynamic	domineering, stubborn, egotistical, tactless, selfish
2	cooperative, service oriented, loving, considerate, humble, patient, diplomatic	shy, vacillating, cowardly, wishy-washy, oversensitive, indefinite
3	expressive, optimistic, imaginative, multitalented, social, creative, enthusiastic	vain, fickle, scattered, critical, egotistical, jealous, wasteful
4	reliable, conservative, methodical, determined, loyal, practical, logical	dogmatic, stubborn, habitual, rigid, argumentative, repressed, resistant
5	persuasive, versatile, courageous, passionate, curious, futuristic, adventurous	overindulgent in the senses, unreliable, inconsistent, moody, irresponsible, careless
6	caring, sympathetic, nurturing, protective, domestic, conscientious, peace loving	self-righteous, vain, sympathetic, overly concerned with others' affairs
7	spiritual, analytical, withdrawn, insightful, philosophical, introspective, truth seeking	reclusive, critical, cold, skeptical, aloof, lonely
8	powerful, money conscious, visionary, authoritative, broadminded, successful, enterprising	egotistical, vain, power and money hungry, materialistic, impatient
9	humanitarian, idealistic, brilliant, creative, generous, futuristic, philanthropic	egocentric, impractical, overemotional, unconcerned
11	The most intuitive of all the numbers, 11 has all the aspects of 2, with leadership capabilities. Elevens must learn how to channel their intuition without falling off center. Spiritual studies help them stay balanced and reach their potential intuitive abilities.	illogical, fanatic
22	The most powerful of the numbers, 22 is the number of the master builder, capable of manifesting an idea in the physical world. Twenty-twos can achieve success by combining the intuitive abilities of 11 and the practicality of 4. They have grand ideas and leadership potential. If 22s do not respond to their inner urges and ideas, they will experience inner conflict.	impractical, lazy, negligent in developing talents

CALCULATING LIFE PATH NUMBERS

The life path number is the most significant number in a numerology chart that helps us understand our life purpose. It is the direction we must follow to align ourselves with our purpose. It describes our life lessons, gifts, and talents and provides the avenue through which we can apply them. To determine a life path number, add the month, day, and year of birth. Reduce and convert the numbers to single-digit numbers and add them up.

For example, if your birth date is March 14, 1980, add 3 (for March, the third month); 5 (14, the date of birth: $1 + 4 = 5$); and 9 (1980, the year of birth: $1 + 9 + 8 + 0 = 18$; $1 + 8 = 9$). The result is 17. Reduce 17: $1 + 7 = 8$. The life path number is 8.

Here's another example based on a birth date of August 27, 1967. Add 8 (for August, the eighth month); 9 (27, the date of birth: $2 + 7 = 9$); and 23 (1967, the year of birth: $1 + 9 + 6 + 7 = 23$; $2 + 3 = 5$). The result is 22. Since 22 is a master number and we do not reduce it, the life path number is 22.

WHAT LIFE PATH NUMBERS REPRESENT

Life Path 1

A born leader. Driven and ambitious, determination allows 1s to fulfill their goals. They need to be in command and like being in the limelight. They place much emphasis on appearance and on maintaining the status quo. They work best in an unconfined atmosphere where they are the boss and have freedom of thought. They need a career where they can lead, such as in business, the military, or government. Developing leadership qualities, drive, and creativity will lead 1s to achieve the success they yearn for. They should avoid becoming too selfish.

Life Path 2

This is the number of the peacemakers due to their sensitivity and desire for cooperation. Twos are diplomatic, tactful, patient, and know how to use these gifts to create harmony among family members and within groups. They have an eye for beauty. Their sensitivity and perception make them good healers. Relationships are important for 2s; their calm demeanor attracts people and they make good companions. Their compassion and understanding can be good in careers such as politics where they can mediate among those with differing opinions, music, architecture, design, and fashion. They are here to follow. Their key to success is learning that they can be effective even when silent. They should watch out for tendencies to avoid confrontation, repress thoughts, and feel hurt too easily.

Life Path 3

Creative, 3s are here to practice self-expression, mainly through creativity. They like to be in the limelight, for example, by showing off artistic abilities. They are sociable and generally happy, optimistic people; they should use their optimism to inspire others. They are emotional and vulnerable. They can channel their abilities into professions such as writing, acting, and music. They should learn focus and discipline to develop their many talents.

Life Path 4

Practical and down to earth, 4s build stability through a step-by-step approach. They are organized, systematic, methodical, committed, and rational. They are hard workers and attain success through much effort. They value justice, honesty, loyalty, and reliability. These qualities make them good marriage partners and successful in fields such as banking, science, and law. They should watch out for tendencies to become too rigid, cautious, and slow at making decisions. Learning flexibility will aid them along this path.

Life Path 5

Variety is the spice of life for 5s who are here to enjoy freedom as well as responsibility. They enjoy anything that brings freedom and adventure, especially travel. They try many things to satisfy their curiosity and their desire for the sensual pleasures in life. They are multitalented and good motivators and can apply their skills to professions such as entertainment, sales, and public service. They should watch for tendencies to be impulsive and irresponsible. Developing discipline and focus will aid them along this path.

Life Path 6

The embodiment of compassion, 6s enjoy being of service to others and can channel this desire into healing and teaching others. They can handle much responsibility and are capable of creating harmony in groups. Their generosity and kindness make them wonderful parents. They also have a creative streak and can excel in music and the arts if they wake up to these abilities and develop them. They would do well to teach others how to be successful rather than help them out of difficult situations: they should watch the tendency to enable others and deprive them of their learning. They should turn their sympathy into empathy; otherwise, they may always attract weak and troubled people.

Life Path 7

Seekers of spiritual truth and wisdom, 7s research all that is related to the occult and spirituality. Their analytical minds help them concentrate, solve problems, and synthesize information. This is a loner path; 7s enjoy solitude and privacy, which is necessary for their search in this lifetime. Marriage will probably not be a priority this lifetime. Good careers that will help develop keen mental powers include research, science, inventive avenues, and anything related to the occult or religion. They must watch out for becoming too isolated and withdrawn, which will lead to loneliness. Learning to express the self more and enjoying the companionship of others can help them maintain balance.

Life Path 8

Seekers of balance between the material and spiritual worlds, including money management, 8s are gifted with good leadership, and management and business sense, which allows them to earn a lot of money. If they do not use their skills they could just as easily experience great financial difficulties. However, through it all they will learn how to wield the physical along with the spiritual. They must avoid becoming too domineering, stubborn, and arrogant. They can channel inspiration and vision into such fields as law, business, finance, management, politics, and teaching.

Life Path 9

The number of completion, 9s have reached the end of a cycle. They are here to combine all the experiences and understandings built thus far to serve humanity on a grand scale. Their desire for a Utopian world drives them toward philanthropic work or anything that improves the world in some way. They are socially conscious humanitarians. They have good imaginations and creative potential. To serve the world they may have to sacrifice for the benefit of others. Letting go of personal desires and attachments allows them to fully channel their efforts to create a better world. They must avoid becoming disillusioned when their ideal of a perfect world does not manifest itself. They are happiest in positions such as teacher, politician, judge, minister, and environmentalist.

Life Path 11 (Master Number)

Channels for insights and spiritual understandings from other realms of existence, 11s dedicate much of their life to working with their intuitive abilities. It is, therefore, important for them to develop confidence in their abilities. Their heightened sensitivity reminds them of their uniqueness. Developing their inner selves will help them feel more confident of their gifts. Their intuitive abilities can best be used in art, religion, inventions, and spiritual avenues. They also possess many of the qualities of 2s, such as cooperation, diplomacy, compassion, and sensitivity. Living up to

59

the potential of a master number carries a great load, so 11s should be careful not to set expectations too high.

Life Path 22 (Master Number)

The most powerful number with the most potential for success, 22s are here as master builders, receptive to the ideas from the higher realms of existence and manifesting them in the physical world. To manifest their dreams, 22s must use their visionary influence to draw people and resources to help them in their efforts. The winning combination is practicality combined with imagination; they are practical visionaries. Their common sense also makes them successful in business and politics. Their ambition moves them to success. They should watch for tendencies to control others. Learning to be more flexible will be beneficial to their growth.

NAMES

Another number that advances us along the life path is the expression number. This number, based on the value of the letters in our full birth name, reveals gifts and talents. It reflects the abilities that come naturally. It also reflects who we are now, as well as the understandings accumulated from past lives. We can look to this number to determine what vocation would best suit us.

The sound of our names has a unique vibration that expresses our style. The names our parents chose for us are no accident: they may have intuitively chosen them to match our energy and essence.

The following chart lists the numerical value of each letter in the alphabet.

1	2	3	4	5	6	7	8	9
A	B	C	D	E	F	G	H	I
J	K	L	M	N	O	P	Q	R
S	T	U	V	W	X	Y	Z	

To find the expression number of your name, write your full birth name, even if you no longer use it, such as in the case of adoptees and married people who assume a spouse's name. Assign the correct numerical value to each letter. Add the values of the first, middle, and last names, and reduce the sum of each to a single digit. Next, add the numbers from each name and reduce the sum to a single digit, except in the case of master numbers.

For example, calculate the expression number for Susan Marie Smith as follows:

Susan = 1 + 3 + 1 + 1 + 5 = 11
Marie = 4 + 1 + 9 + 9 + 5 = 28 = 2 + 8 = 10 = 1 + 0 = 1
Smith = 1 + 4 + 9 + 2 + 8 = 24 = 2 + 4 = 6
Total: 11 + 1 + 6 = 18 = 1 + 8 = 9

EXPRESSION NUMBERS

Expression 1

Natural leaders, independent, ambitious, and courageous explorers who are not afraid of taking risks. They work best as their own boss. They have strength, perseverance, and lots of willpower. They must look at themselves honestly and acknowledge parts of the self that are unproductive. They need to watch tendencies to become too self-centered, opinionated, prideful, and domineering. They benefit by learning to cooperate with others.

Expression 2

Cooperative and good team workers, they strive for balance and peace in their relations. They are intuitive and sensitive. Their friendly and supportive nature makes them good mates. They must avoid tendencies to experience vicariously the thoughts and feelings of those around them due to their heightened sensitivity.

Expression 3

They are expressive, outgoing, and positive. They have strong creative streaks and are here to develop their self-expression to the maximum. Their imagination, as well as writing and verbal skills, are great assets that may be channeled into careers as artists or entertainers. They benefit by learning to focus their energies in one area, and set and fulfill goals.

Expression 4

They are systematic, methodical, and organized, with a good understanding of structure, and can use these skills to build a strong foundation. They are reliable, responsible, honest, sincere, and trustworthy. They can see a project through to the end and are good at jobs that require mental acumen. Their determination and steadfastness will help create success. They need to watch tendencies to be too rigid, stubborn, and workaholic. They would benefit by becoming more imaginative and having more fun in life.

Expression 5

They like freedom and change and are adaptable. Their versatile and multitalented nature makes them good travelers. They like to take risks and always seek new adventures. Their curiosity encourages them to taste a little bit of all that life offers. They need to watch tendencies to become too self-indulgent. Learning self-discipline and completion will help in life. They are people oriented and do well in jobs such as sales.

Expression 6

They are loving and caring nurturers with the ability to comfort and aid others, making them exceptional parents, teachers, healers, and counselors. Their desire to improve the world and the human condition can cause them to meddle too much in others' lives, perhaps depriving others of their lessons. Learning to empower others will benefit all concerned. They also have a creative streak that will require pulling away from aiding others so to focus on developing their talents.

Expression 7

They have analytical and logical minds, delving into the mysteries of the world and seeking spiritual wisdom. They crave much knowledge in this lifetime and often spend time alone researching and studying. They are perfectionists; it would behoove them to become experts in one area rather than scattering energies in many different directions. They will need to watch for tendencies to be too much of an introvert, to hide from the world, and to be dishonest.

Expression 8

They are here to be the best they can be and achieve balance between the spiritual and material worlds. They have an inner drive to be leaders and may possess a competitive edge. During this lifetime they face issues with money, authority, and power. They are ambitious and remain steadfast in their ideals despite many challenges and ups and downs. Their dynamism and vision will aid them in manifesting their desires.

Expression 9

With a grand vision for aiding the world, requiring them to go beyond their egos and sacrificing personal ambitions, they are here to serve and improve the world. They may sometimes be so focused on world causes that they may forget to give affection to those closest to them or even give themselves what they need. Since the number 9 represents the completion of a cycle, they are here to bring to fruition all they have built in previous lives and achieve a level of mastery during this lifetime.

Expression 11 (Master Number)

Individuals with this number have the gift of extreme sensitivity and intuition. They are very open to messages from their inner selves. They must ground and balance themselves to remain clear channels for all the information coming to them. They may have noticed these abilities as children; their childhood could have been difficult because of their unusual abilities. They can be excellent teachers due to their inspiration and vision. They need to balance emotional extremes.

Expression 22 (Master Number)

The number 22 is a master number with great potential. Those with this expression number are master builders who are here to fulfill a grand mission. They have the ability to manifest their ideas in the physical world due to a combination of practicality and vision. They are aware of the great task they have to fulfill, which at times can be intimidating to the point of causing them to shy away from their big plans. They are not here to satisfy themselves with accomplishing only small goals. They must go beyond fear to take the risks necessary to accomplish big plans. Since the 22 can be reduced to 4, they may also possess rigidity, making them too methodical in their approach. To fulfill their mission they must go beyond the narrow limitations of the number 4 and take the necessary risks to be leaders and manifesters of grand visions.

DATE OF BIRTH

The day we were born is significant because it reveals the special gifts and talents that can help us move toward our life path. Our date of birth affects us in a manner similar to our Ascendant in astrology, reflecting how we approach the world and appear to others. Your birth date number can be studied as a single-digit number as well as a double-digit number. For example, with a birth date of 18, use both 18 and 9 (1 + 8 = 9). The double-digit number reveals qualities in addition to those described by the single-digit number.

HIDDEN PASSION NUMBER

Numbers that appear more than once in a name represent talents and abilities. The most frequently occurring number, or numbers, represents our Hidden Passion Number (or numbers), which reveals a talent that we are passionate about. Expressing our talents is a means by which we can align ourselves with our life purpose. (For example, in the name Tim Roy Smith, the number that appears most frequently is 9 (the value of I, R, and I). So his hidden passion is to be a leader, a humanitarian who leads the world toward a new vision.)

HEART'S DESIRE (SOUL URGE NUMBER)

To further understand our desires we can look to the Heart's Desire, or Soul Urge Number, which describes our innermost desires and explains many of our motivations and choices in life. If we do not express this soul urge, we cannot be completely fulfilled. To find this number, total the numerical values of the vowels of your full name. Do not reduce master numbers.

PLANES OF EXPRESSION

There are four modes (planes of expression) of experiencing life: mental, physical, emotional, and intuitive. Our most dominant plane (the plane with the highest numerical value) represents the way we experience and respond to life. It also shows where our gifts and talents lie. We can make better choices when we rely on the mode represented by our dominant plane. Planes with small numerical value show areas that need developing.

Each letter of the alphabet falls within one of the four modes (see chart). To complete a planes of expression chart and see your predominant modes of expression, place the letters of your name in the correct categories. For example, if your name were SAM, you would place the letter "S" in Emotional-Vacillating box; the letter "A" in the Mental-Creative box; and the letter "M" in the Physical-Balanced box.

	Creative	Vacillating	Balanced
Physical	E	W	D M
Mental	A	H J N P	G L
Emotional	I O R Z	B S T X	
Intuitive	K	F Q U Y	C V

Here's an example: If my name had seven letters in the mental plane, one in the emotional plane, and four in the intuitive plane, the dominance would be in the mental plane. Therefore, I would do well to rely on my intellect and intuition. Further developing the physical and emotional planes would bring greater balance.

KARMA

Having uncovered our gifts and talents, we must next delve into the lessons we need to learn to complete our life purpose. Hidden in a name are the karmic lessons a soul will experience during this lifetime. Karma represents the awarenesses we lack within ourselves. Interestingly enough, we find our karma in numerology by identifying the numbers that are missing in our names. Those who have long names that contain all the numbers have developed many skills and abilities in past lives. Well-rounded people like this find success fairly easy to attain since they have few obstacles to overcome.

People with long names containing only a few numbers find they are talented in a specific area and do best by focusing all their energies in that area. The more numbers that are missing in a name, the more obstacles and challenges will be encountered.

To find your karmic lessons, write your complete birth name, assigning the correct numerical value to each letter. Use the chart in the "Names" section. Missing numbers indicate your karmic lessons. The universe will bring lessons to help you learn; it is up to you how you will handle them.

For example, find the karmic lessons for Patrick David Lee:

Patrick: 7, 1, 2, 9, 9, 3, 2
David: 4, 1, 4, 9, 4
Lee: 3, 5, 5

The missing numbers are 6 and 8, each one representing a karmic lesson.

KARMIC LESSONS: MISSING NUMBERS

Karmic Lesson 1

You need to show more initiative and determination, and stand up for your ideas. Learn independence, how to make your own decisions, and how to assert yourself. Increase self-confidence by working to overcome fears. You face many decisions in this lifetime.

Karmic Lesson 2

You need to learn diplomacy, tact, patience, and how to cooperate with others. Detach from the need to receive rewards for your work: this will help you learn the balance and sensitivity of the number 2.

Karmic Lesson 3

You are self-critical and perfectionistic; you have a difficult time living up to your own standards. You are often too serious and would benefit by being less self-critical, being more optimistic, and learning to enjoy life more. Your low self-confidence often inhibits your full self-expression.

Karmic Lesson 4

You need to overcome confusion by learning discipline and how to take small steps towards building a foundation. Learning focus and concentration, combined with practicality and organization, will help you in life. You have avoided work and the necessary steps for building a foundation, so during this lifetime you must avoid shortcuts and engage in productive activities.

Karmic Lesson 5

Overcome fears by being more adventurous. You can broaden your vision through travel and by being open to new experiences. Embrace change to overcome inflexibility and rigidity. You will be more comfortable with your life when you learn to adapt. In the past, you have avoided experiences and, therefore, lack a broad understanding of life. In this incarnation, you must learn from your experiences and take some risks.

Karmic Lesson 6

You have difficulty committing and being responsible to others. You feel isolated and alone when you do not open up emotionally and show your true self. Go beyond superficiality and build meaningful relationships where you can share your true thoughts. You must let go of fears regarding responsibility and be of service to others.

Karmic Lesson 7

You are here to learn to focus your knowledge and talents in one area so you can develop your abilities to reach your potential. To accomplish this you must go beyond superficial understanding of things. You are here to develop your spiritual nature, which has been avoided in the past. Learning to think logically will aid you along this path.

Karmic Lesson 8

You are here to learn how to manage money. Until this is learned you may experience many difficulties with financial matters. You are very independent and have difficulty with authority figures. Learning to balance the material and spiritual aspects of life will help you understand the energy flow of money and how to deal with authority.

Karmic Lesson 9

You are here to learn compassion, tolerance, and understanding. You need to learn how to commit to a goal or project that aids the community or the world at large. You would do well to broaden your vision and realize your potential to influence others. In the past, you have avoided committing to humanitarian causes; learning to accept and channel your emotions can help you connect with people and fulfill your mission.

CHALLENGE NUMBERS

As with karmic lessons, challenge numbers reveal our weak areas, those in which we will encounter many lessons. Challenges are gifts in disguise because they represent lessons from the universe that can help us evolve. The sooner we are aware of these challenges—and when they occur—the better we'll be able to understand and surmount them.

We encounter four main challenges throughout our lifetime, each one influencing us at different times. The first challenge begins early in life and continues to the early part of the middle of life. The transition to the second challenge occurs as the first one is completed, during the middle part of life. We feel the most intense challenge, the third one, throughout our lifetime. The fourth challenge begins in the last part of life and continues until the end of life.

CALCULATING CHALLENGE NUMBERS

Use the following process to calculate challenge numbers. For example, if your birth date is September 28, 1980, write the month, day, and year as single digits. September = 9; 28 = 1 (2 + 8 = 10; 1 + 0 = 1); 1983 = 3 (1 + 9 + 8 + 3 = 21; 2 + 1 = 3). Master numbers are reduced.

1. Determine the first challenge number by subtracting the smaller of the month and day from the larger of the two: 9 – 1 = **8**.
2. Figure the second challenge number by subtracting the smaller of the day and year from the larger of the two: 3 – 1 = **2**.
3. Calculate the third challenge number by subtracting the smaller of the first and second challenge numbers from the larger of the two: 8 – 2 = **6**.

Finally, ascertain the fourth challenge number by subtracting the smaller of the month and year from the larger of the two: 9 – 3 = 6.

Challenge 0

The challenge is to respond to the needs of society. For those having avoided service in the past, there will be many opportunities in this lifetime to serve others in need. Happiness and fulfillment come through service and help to others.

Challenge 1

The challenge is to be independent and self-assertive. For those having too often run with the crowd, in the past, at the expense of beliefs and values, there will be situations presenting the opportunity to be leaders, and expressing personal views, even if they disagree with those of the majority. The more such people practice independence, self-reliance, and standing up for their beliefs, the happier they will be.

Challenge 2

The challenge is to gain emotional balance by controlling oversensitivity and the tendency to pick up and vicariously experience other people's emotions. The closer in touch with who we are and the greater the risk we're willing to take in expressing ourselves, the more balanced and centered we become. We need to use intuition and compassion for the benefit of others.

Challenge 3

To build up self-confidence in creative abilities and increase self-worth, we must overcome self-doubt and criticism. The more real we become and the more we express who we are, the easier it will be to relate to other people and feel connected, rather than isolated and alone.

Challenge 4

The challenge is to learn organization and to build a foundation one step at a time to achieve success. To achieve success we must learn practicality and follow through on commitments. Fulfillment will come when we apply the stability of the number 4 to manifest ideas in the physical world.

Challenge 5

The challenge is stay focused and not to explore every whim and desire for new experiences. We're tempted by many sensual pleasures, so we must learn moderation. We can achieve happiness by learning the value of discipline and the joy of committing to something.

Challenge 6

The challenge is to be more accepting of others, even if they do not quite measure up to our high standards. Opening our minds to include other viewpoints and perspectives will help us be more expansive and accepting. We can also overcome the tendency to be self-righteous by being of service to others through teaching or healing.

Challenge 7

Skepticism and doubt of anything that cannot be logically proved keep us distanced from the spiritual side of life. The challenge is to embrace feelings and intuition and explore the spiritual side of life. There will be opportunities to develop faith. The more we allow faith to break down the barriers to the inner self and emotions, the happier we will be.

Challenge 8

The challenge is to achieve a balance between spiritual and physical goals. When the drive to attain physical wealth and prosperity overshadow spiritual development, happiness will elude us. Until we learn to put our material ambitions into proper perspective, we will be faced with financial challenges. When we master the energies of the number 8, we will understand how to be "in the world but not of it."

TYING IT TOGETHER WITH BRIDGE NUMBERS

How successfully we use the energies of our numerology chart is determined by how well we make them work together harmoniously. By studying the relationship among the numbers in the numerology chart, we can see how to achieve this. If we suppress the energy of any of these numbers, we will experience frustration, perhaps leading to "dis-ease" in the body. For example, someone with expression number 3, which instills the desire to be social and outgoing, may be creative and tend to be scattered. With a soul urge number of 7, the challenge would be to blend the desire for solitude and privacy (to explore the inner depths of the mind and universe) with the outgoing and social quality.

A bridge number—the difference between the larger and smaller numbers—helps us create harmony between two numbers with a balancing energy. For example, the bridge number for the expression number 3 and the soul urge number 7 is 4 (7 – 3 = 4), indicating the need for stability and practicality. Remember, challenges represent areas of tremendous growth potential. In this example, working with the energies of the two numbers can help to achieve balance and avoid extremes (such as becoming a recluse). It is recommended to bridge the most significant numbers on your chart, such as the life path and expression, and life path and heart's desire number.

Ideally, our expression number supports our life path goals. Five, the bridge number between a life path number of 7 and an expression number of 2, says to lighten up and seek more fun and adventure. To satisfy an urge to be a cooperative, relationship-oriented person (2), one needs to be more lighthearted and enjoy life (5) rather than engaging in lone activities (7). With two of the same numbers expressing the same energy, no bridging is needed.

As we share our gifts and talents on our life path, we must seek to avoid being stymied by our karmic lessons and challenges. We can set ourselves up for success by being aware of our lessons and giving ourselves enough time and space to learn them before putting them to the test.

CYCLES

What steps should we take to fulfill our life purpose? How do we know when it is time to act, or to sit back and formulate a plan? Which lessons should we focus on now? Our lives run in cycles of nine years. Each year brings its own energies, influences, and lessons. A cycle begins with a personal year 1, indicating new beginnings where we foster new ideas. The cycle ends with year 9, the year of completion and transformation as we assimilate all that we've built during the last eight years.

To calculate your personal year, add the day and month of your birth to the current year. For example, for the year 2002, a person born on March 3 would calculate his personal year as follows:

1. Add March: 3
2. Add day of birth: 3
3. Add the numbers in the current year: 2002 = 2 + 0 + 0 + 2 = 4.
4. Add the results: 3+ 3 + 4= 10= 1+0=1.

In 2002, a person born on March 3 would be in personal year 1. Their next personal year would begin January 1 of 2003.

The following summarizes the energies of each year. For additional insight, study the Qualities of Numbers Chart earlier in this chapter.

Year 1: Set new ideas into motion, make changes, and embark on a new direction.
Year 2: Build important relationships and develop ideas started in year 1.
Year 3: Add creativity to the ideas started in year 1.
Year 4: Work hard and stay disciplined to achieve results.
Year 5: Adapt an attitude of freedom and expectancy: this is a year of unpredictability.

Year 6: Serve and practice responsibility.
Year 7: Pursue spiritual study and personal growth.
Year 8: Reap the benefits of efforts and gain recognition for accomplishments.
Year 9: Complete all that has transpired over the last eight years. Let go of what no longer serves. Prepare to start fresh in year 1.

A Born Leader

Agnes Gonxha Bojaxhiu was born August 27, 1910. She was a determined person, overcoming opposition from religious leaders and politicians. She remained committed to helping India's poor and sick, even though it meant living apart from her family, often in horrendous conditions. She found unique approaches to problems and had the courage to follow her own path, earning the attention and respect of the entire world: her life path number "1" reveals that she was destined to become a leader; she used the assets of her birth date of 27 to inspire others.

As she followed this path, she also allowed her self-expression number 7 to blossom. Through her study of Catholicism, she searched for the meaning of life and death. She remained devoted to God and paved a spiritual path for others to follow. Her analytical mind and deep insights about life led people throughout the world to seek her advice.

She successfully bridged her life path and expression number (6) by applying the energy of 6: love and service. Mother Teresa embodied the qualities of love, compassion, and generosity.

TASKS

Follow the instructions in this chapter to calculate your entire numerology chart. In most cases, remember to reduce two-digit numbers, except for the master numbers 11 and 22. Fill in the blanks in the chart to create your record.

Life Path Number (month + day + year of birth):

Expression Number (based on full name):

Hidden Passion Number (most frequently occurring number in name):

Soul Urge Number (based on vowels in full name):

Planes of Expression:

Karmic Lessons (based on missing numbers in full name):

Challenge Numbers
1 (difference between day and month of birth):

2 (difference between day and year of birth):

3 (difference between the first two challenge numbers):

4 (difference between month and year of birth):

Personal Year (day + month of birth + current year):

1. To increase your proficiency, create a numerology chart for a friend.
2. Prepare a numerology chart for someone you are close to. Compare this chart to yours and use the information to better understand the energies between you. Have you discovered why you get along in certain areas? Why you disagree on certain subjects? What strengths does each of you have that you can share and teach? Look for similarities in your karmic debt numbers. There is often an attraction to people who have similar lessons. Do you have similar lessons?
3. Make a collage representing your numerology makeup.
4. List ways you can fulfill your numerological potential.

QUESTIONS

1. To which numbers have you ever been drawn?
2. Why do you like or dislike your name? What names do you like?
3. What numbers have been significant and brought you good fortune in this lifetime?
4. How do you feel or react when someone uses your nickname or other name?
5. To what extent does your career allow you to express your life path number?
6. To what extent do you embody the energies of your expression number?
7. To what extent are you living up to the potential of your life path number?
8. To what degree have you surmounted your challenge numbers?
9. How have you experienced your karmic lessons?

EXERCISES

1. Describe how the following influences interact to help you fulfill your life purpose: life path and expression numbers; expression and soul urge numbers; expression and hidden passion numbers; life path and hidden passion numbers.
2. Use a different name for a day or for a week. Notice any changes and record them: when your name changes so does the vibration. Calculate the new numerology chart for your nickname and see if what it describes is true for you.

3. Refer to your life path and personal expression numbers. Describe how you are fulfilling your life purpose. List ways to be more in alignment with your soul's assignment and set up goals to accomplish this.

4. Calculate your challenge numbers. Examine your past and reflect on how those challenges came into your life, at what times, and how you dealt with them. Challenge number 3 is with you for life. Imagine ways you can work with this challenge and turn it into a strength.

5. Study your karmic lesson numbers. Reflect on how these lessons came to you and how you dealt with them. Write a plan for learning these lessons. How can you incorporate these understandings? For example, if your karmic number is 1, you can focus on ways to build independence and leadership.

6. Calculate your personal year number for the last three years. To what degree were you in harmony with the energies of those years? For example, if you were in a year 1, did you begin lots of new projects? If you were in a year 7, did you devote a lot of time to yourself and to spiritual/self growth issues?

7. Calculate your personal year number for the current year. List ways you can harmonize with the energies of this year.

Five

Rayid Iris: What the Eyes Reveal

Streamlined for Action

Patrick was a student of spiritual study at the school I attended. Eager to learn more about himself, he couldn't wait to explore Rayid iris.

When Patrick learned that his core iris structure was a stream, he was amazed that it corresponded to an earlier intuitive reading, which described him as a river that sometimes moves swiftly like a stream. Patrick, in fact, embodies the stream qualities of calm, balance, and intuition.

Learning more about the gifts and talents of the stream vibration helped Patrick prepare himself for success. To develop his innate healing abilities, he took a part-time job at a chiropractic office and began learning some healing techniques. He wanted to develop his own body—he possessed the endless energy typical of a stream—as well as its grace and ease, and recognized his capacity to learn kinesthetically. Combining these talents, Patrick became a Tai Chi instructor.

Through Rayid iris, Patrick learned that he had to keep the stream moving. He faced the challenge of dealing with change, often slow to happen. This quality again paralleled an intuitive reading, which described his tendency to procrastinate, thus slowing his progress.

At the spiritual school where he was studying, Patrick was frustrated at the slow pace of the classes. He visualized steady progress, and was soon invited to attend the next series of classes.

Patrick began to take greater risks to fulfill his dreams. When his position at work was eliminated, he did freelance computer work while focusing on two of his dreams: writing a book and pursuing a career in public speaking. He left the small college town of Champaign, Illinois, and moved back to Chicago, where he began to write his book and polish his public speaking.

Our eyes—the windows to the soul—tell a remarkable story about who we are. Like fingerprints, each iris has a unique and particular pattern. The study of the iris is called "Rayid." "Ray" refers to light and "id" is the ego, so it symbolizes the illumination into the ego. Personality traits, gifts and talents, strengths and weaknesses, fears and lessons, are all revealed in the eyes. Eyes also reveal how we experience life and express ourselves, either through the emotions, through the mind, kinesthetically, or through the polarities of emotion and mind. The influences revealed by the eyes bring us the lessons we need to fulfill our life purpose. When we are unaware of the influences acting on us, we remain controlled by unconscious tendencies, habits, and limitations.

Rayid is a powerful guidepost on the path to self-awareness because it takes us to the point of origin of many of our behaviors. All the traits and influence of thought patterns revealed in the eyes are inherited from our ancestors. Traits in the left eye derive from the mother's side of the family; traits from the right eye come from the father's side. We can research our family tree to see where, how, and perhaps why certain iris patterns were formed. Self-awareness allows us to break free of family patterns and become the people we are meant to be.

As a self-empowerment tool, Rayid reveals our life potential and points us toward our life purpose. Similar to astrological influences, iris traits exist to help us learn and grow in a conscious, aware fashion. The more we are aware of these influences, the better able we are to work with them. As with cooking, the more we know about how flavors compliment each other, the more skilled we are in preparing delicious dishes. When we know our strengths we can build upon them and choose avenues in life where those strengths can shine. Likewise, when we are aware of areas of weakness or challenges, we can use tools to help us strengthen these areas and turn them into gifts.

The traits expressed through our eyes are not meant to put us into some rigidly defined category. They are forms of expression, representing our potential, to work with in this lifetime. It is our choice how we work with these influences. We are vibrant and capable of changing and becoming whatever we desire. "The iris is a map of the personality. It can show you how to find your true self, but that is all. It does not define you. Reach beyond the iris to your true self. Go beyond limitations of your personality. And remember that the part of you that knows who you *really* are will never need any training, any information and never did."[1]

Rayid teaches that to embody our wholeness, we must assimilate the qualities of all the different iris types. When we can allow ourselves to express and feel life through all the different modalities—mental, emotional, kinesthetic, and extremist—we will be balanced. As Denny Johnson states, "Ultimately, each of us will be able to gain access to all of the levels of consciousness represented by the Stream, Jewel, Flower and Shaker structures, and to move freely from one way of being to another. This is the wholeness that we seek."[2]

No eye pattern is better than another; each offers specific strengths, gifts, and talents. Denny Johnson explains, "Every position in the eye is a gift; don't think in terms of 'getting rid' of an area's influence. Regard all traits as positive attributes. They are not just some transgenerational garbage that is there simply to be weeded out. They are not just problems to be coped with; they are pointers to how we can grow and change. They are there to facilitate a long-term evolution of consciousness.

"There is an unconscious mechanism that automatically gives us the lessons we need in order to move toward wholeness. If we find these lessons uncomfortable, we can choose to understand their value and to learn them in a conscious way instead."[3]

A thorough Rayid iris analysis includes a description of the four core iris constitutions (structures): Flower, Jewel, Stream, and Shaker. The description reveals the vibrational pattern of how we experience life, gifts and talents, strengths and weaknesses, fears, challenges, communication style, and life purpose. Rayid iris also covers:

1. Whether we have right- or left-brain dominance.
2. Whether we tend to be more introverted or extroverted.

3. Identification of ring patterns and what they mean.
4. Iris markings, their location, and their meaning.

There are four different iris constitutions: Flower, Jewel, Stream, and Shaker, as well as combinations: Shaker-Flower, Stream-Jewel, Stream-Flower, and Shaker-Jewel. The Jewel (mental quality) and Flower (emotional quality) are opposite energies. When they are combined, they form either the Shaker or Stream iris. When the mental and emotional energies harmonize, they create the Stream, which is calming and stable. However, if the energies repel each other, they form the Shaker iris, which is extremist, unstable, and constantly in motion.

THE FOUR CONSTITUTIONS

Flower (Emotional)

Flowers are emotional and creative people who experience life predominantly through their feelings and emotions. They are changeable and flexible and, therefore, need to learn organization, completion, focus, and commitment. These qualities help them choose something and stick with it until completion. Flowers have great creative abilities and would do well to channel these talents into the arts, dance, music, or the entertainment world. They like to be admired for their work and enjoy being around people so they can express their innate joy and vision.

Flowers often fall into a pattern of looking for ways to fill themselves up, going from one thing to the next hoping to find fulfillment. They can remain in this search until they realize that true fulfillment does not come from an outer source; rather, it comes from the inside. Filling themselves with spirituality and a belief in a higher being, and loving and valuing oneself brings them fulfillment. Since they live life through the emotions they can be reactionary and look to other people and situations to blame. The key for them is to understand the thoughts that cause their emotions. They find answers when they recognize themselves as the cause for everything that occurs in their life.

Jewel (Mental)

Jewels experience life mostly from a mental perspective, taking in information and analyzing and synthesizing it. Jewels have analytical minds; when balanced and focused, they can offer clarity of thought. Due to their stability, good verbal skills, ability to set and achieve goals and ambition, they make good leaders. They may attempt to control others and the environment. However, they dislike to be controlled and seek freedom for themselves. Their minds are intense. They are opinionated and always think they are right, closing themselves off to other viewpoints.

Jewels are drawn to their opposite, Flowers. They want to learn about emotions—an area in which they are uncomfortable and unfamiliar—from Flowers. They want intimacy, yet are afraid to immerse themselves in it because it would require surrender and vulnerability, difficult to do for mental types.

Therefore, relationships with Flowers can be good for Jewels as they open up to their emotions and learn to "flow" with life, rather than be rigid. The key for Jewels is to master the mind so the mind does not become their master. This does not mean hours of analysis; rather, they can achieve knowing through trusting themselves. They excel in jobs that require detail, a focused mind, stability, and leadership.

Stream (Kinesthetic)

These sensitive and intuitive people bring peace, calm, and balance to all areas of life, including relationships. Therefore, they make good mediators because they can identify with both the mental and emotional types (Stream is a blend of both these qualities). People—especially Shakers who need to learn moderation—are drawn to them for their stable and healing presence.

With their heightened sensitivity, these folks need to be careful not to experience vicariously other people's thoughts and feelings and lose their identity. They can channel their abundant physical energy and nurturing qualities to professions such as the healing arts, athletics, bodywork, and counseling.

Streams experience life kinesthetically: their body and senses are the avenues through which they integrate and learn from their experiences. They can learn much from Shakers, their opposite, such as how to embrace change and how to initiate. Shakers often bring excitement to Streams, who need outside stimulation to enliven them, while Streams offer support and stability to Shakers.

Shaker (Extremist)

These dynamic, enthusiastic, vital individuals are here to change the world. They have insightful, often radical, ideas about how the world can be, and work towards implementing these changes. They approach all they do with zeal and joy, which makes them magnets for other people.

Shakers have both mental (Jewel) and emotional (Flower) qualities. The interaction of these energies makes them dynamic. They must be careful not to swing too much to either extreme, which can lead them down dark roads, such as drug and alcohol abuse, or misuse of power and authority. They would do well to learn stability and balance, and ground themselves in their bodies through appropriate diet and exercise. They can learn these qualities from Streams, their opposite.

These folks need a free, unstructured life to implement their cutting-edge ideas. When they harness their ambition and drive, they can become great leaders, inventors, or scientists who pave new roads for future generations.

The four constitutions: Flower, Jewel, Stream, Shaker

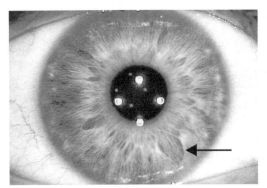

Flower

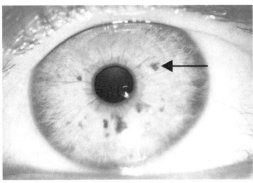

Jewel

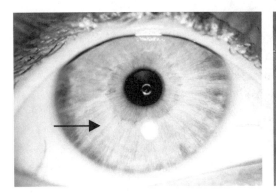

Stream

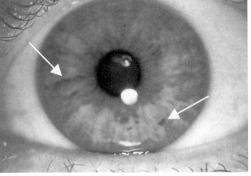

Shaker

COMBINATIONS

Shaker-Jewel

Behind revolutionary upheavals and major inventions and discoveries, we usually find a Shaker-Jewel. The powerful combination of Shaker dynamism and enthusiasm and the mental acumen and keenness of Jewel helps them blaze the trails and burn through convention to new vistas. In order to carry out their grand visions they require one thing: freedom. They hate to be bound by rules, authorities, and structures that put a damper on their active minds.

Their futuristic ideas are often rejected by society so they may have to walk the path alone. Being alone does not bother this loner type; in fact, it allows them to spend more time finding ways to implement their ideas. They must watch the tendency, however, to become too reclusive and introspective. They have the Shaker tendency to swing between extremes, so they need to be grounded in the physical world. At the height of their potential these folks make excellent leaders. Cultivating more compassion and empathy helps them in their leadership roles and in personal relationships.

Shaker-Flower

Shaker-Flowers have unconventional ideas about how to improve the world—and the zeal to change it—coupled with the emotional expression of the Flower. They want to bring their futuristic plans for progress to fruition and to be recognized when they do this. Cultivating their dynamism and using their emotions is a draw for others to join them in their quest for change. Good leaders, they inspire groups of people, but they must control their use of power and their mood swings if they are to be effective. They must also focus their attention because the urge to be a force for change often leads them in too many directions at once. When they master these tendencies, they can channel their passion to manifest their visions and transform the world.

In relationships, they deal with fears of being alone, which may lead them to manipulate their partners. Control issues also may be a source of friction in personal relationships and other areas of their lives.

Stream-Jewel

These folks embody caring, compassion, and wisdom. Their mental side (Jewel) has given them good minds that they like to keep active by reading and researching various sources of information. They are good at organizing this information into an understandable system. They are also capable of bringing groups of people together.

Their kinesthetic (Stream) qualities give them the compassion, intuition, stability, and strength to counsel other people and nurture their families They can combine these talents to become exceptional teachers, healers, and parents.

These people often want to take control and would do well to surrender this need. They would thus ease self-imposed pressure to be perfect and stop judging themselves and others.

Stream-Flower

These folks are here to bring compassion, sensitivity, and beauty to the world. They accomplish this with their physical presence (attractive bodies and nice clothes), their home (decorated in fine taste), and their careers, which may involve some form of creativity (chefs, artists, decorators).

Stream-Flowers are blessed with creativity and emotional connection (Flower) and the strength and sensitivity of Stream, making them very balanced individuals. Their balance and compassion also make them good parents. They must keep their sensitivity and desire for material possessions in check so they are not pulled off center in either area.

INTROVERSION AND EXTROVERSION

Now that we've explored core constitutions, we'll consider the effect of introversion and extroversion on the personality.

Introversion

Introverts are typically quiet and spend more time listening than talking. Through their years of listening and observing, these individuals gather a lot of wisdom. Their quietude is not a sign of unhappiness. Quite the contrary: they can be content individuals with the power to be introspective, with a keen imagination and a strong sense of inner security. Their gifts include empathy, integration, stability, and appreciation. The lessons for the introvert include being truthful and decisive, and learning to honestly and openly express the self. They are sensitive and tolerant individuals.

Extroversion

Extroverts are outgoing, boisterous, and expressive individuals. These vital and energetic people are social and enjoy all types of human interaction at work and at play. They like to channel their energy into many endeavors, always looking to produce something. You can count on an extrovert to be open and honest. However, sometimes their brute honesty can hurt those who are more sensitive. In their urge to create, extroverts can become impatient and must relax. Extroverts are gifted with practicality, forthrightness, and the ability to achieve. The lessons for them include patience, respect, and stillness.

HEMISPHERIC DOMINANCE

Each side of the body corresponds to the cerebral hemisphere (right or left brain) on the opposite side. For example, the left eye corresponds to the right brain and the right eye corresponds to the left brain. To determine your dominant hemisphere, determine which eye has more traits.

The right brain is associated with the more feminine polarity—the emotions, feelings, creativity, and the inner self. Those with right-brain dominance have fertile imaginations and enjoy philosophy. They need to focus and manifest their imaginative ideas in the physical world. They are social, relaxed people who are comfortable in many social situations. Among other qualities, right-brain people are social, gregarious, receptive, creative, imaginative, intuitive, spontaneous, and feminine. Negative tendencies include avoidance, disorganization, and impracticality.

The left brain is associated with the masculine tendencies of logical thinking, control, decision making, practicality, and how one communicates. Left-brain people are generally logical, organized, decisive, traditional, high achievers, good communicators, aggressive, and more masculine, factual, assertive, and goal oriented. They have the groundedness to turn plans into reality. One of their gifts is the ability to communicate clearly. Negative tendencies include too much emphasis on materialism, skepticism, possessiveness, controlling behavior, insensitivity, and slowness to change.

RINGS IN THE IRIS

We next look at rings in the iris, which may or may not be present. They add a new dimension to the person, and modify the core iris constitution. There are four types of rings that may be present: Ring of Harmony, Ring of Freedom, Ring of Purpose, and Ring of Determination.

Ring of Harmony

People with a harmony ring have a strong desire to heal the world. In their quest to bring about peace and love, they may join philanthropic organizations and fight for causes to improve the environment. They are sensitive and empathetic individuals who set high ideals for themselves and for others. People with this ring can achieve success by calling on their power of influence, setting boundaries, and learning when to say no, which helps them to keep from being taken advantage of. They tend to take on too many things at once and wear themselves out. Getting appropriate rest and spending time healing themselves will do much to make these people more effective in the world.

When people with harmony patterns achieve internal balance, they can influence others by their healing presence. What needs to be healed is the feeling of not being supported, a feeling that began while still in the womb. Such feelings originated with the mother, feeling unsupported in her environment, who passed these feelings to the child. To avoid pain, people develop the pattern of keeping busy all the time. Those with harmony patterns have a hard time slowing down, so their lesson is to relax, rejuvenate, and heal themselves.

They can be most successful when they influence many people without exhausting themselves. Working with large groups of people in areas such as teaching and lecturing is one solution. Another challenge for those with harmony patterns is to overcome the tendency to take on the problems of others, or assume all the responsibility when there is a problem. Other factors that help people with harmony rings are creating a peaceful and tranquil living environment, practicing stillness, deep breathing, meditation, and singing.

Harmony ring people can become depressed and cynical when they find the world is not measuring up to their high ideals. Realizing that true healing occurs first within themselves can change this tendency. Once this is accomplished, they can heal the world with their wonderful gifts.

Ring of Freedom

This ring is concerned with freedom and achievement. People with this ring have the gift of being able to realize their goals and be productive. They have a drive to achieve and, luckily, have a lot of energy to channel towards fulfilling their goals. It is important for them to channel energy towards the fulfillment of some goal, otherwise, their excess energy will become nervous tension and stress, or they may become impatient and cast aside anyone who procrastinates.

They like freedom and tend to rebel against authority and hierarchical systems. The ring indicates a break with the current generation, perhaps due to divorce, single-parent families, or parents who do not share much love. This creates a negative outlook on relationships. This pattern is the polar opposite of the harmony ring patterns, which are overly empathetic, while the freedom patterns lack empathy. Each can reach balance by assimilating qualities of the other. The key to success is to channel their energies into beautiful creations in an unstructured environment.

Ring of Purpose

People with this ring know they are here to fulfill an important mission; their life is focused on finding out just what exactly that mission is. Finding their purpose may be quite challenging because they have trouble translating their goals and ideals into reality. They also need to realize that choosing a purpose will not limit them. They will actually feel a sense of relief and fulfillment when they finally find their purpose and form goals to fulfill it. They can then be creative in finding ways to express their purpose. Commitment to their purpose is what will help these individuals move away from procrastination and egocentrism. They must be decisive to move forward. Focusing their attention on the present and, of course, doing self-awareness work will help them find their purpose.

Ring of Determination

This is one of the rings that usually develops at age 50 or later. As we grow older, the ring develops in response to increasing decisiveness and rigidity. The wishy-washy behavior of youth is replaced by firm opinions and the confidence to speak them. The negative tendency of people who have developed this ring is to become inflexible and stubborn. They may be closed to new ideas and other viewpoints. Behind their resistance to change is a clinging to the past and old patterns. By keeping the mind active, there will be no time to stagnate and live in the past. Spiritual study will also help them transcend mental rigidity by moving beyond narrow thinking and offering challenging and thought-provoking experiences.

POSITIONAL IRIS TRAITS

Similar to an astrological wheel divided into 12 houses, each house representing a particular area of life (self-development, family, career, etc.), the eyes are divided into different areas of expression. Each trait (Jewel, Flower, Stream) governs a different mode of behavior (similar to the 12 signs of the zodiac and the 10 planets) and falls within a certain place in the iris (similar to the 12 zodiacal houses). The traits show the type of behavior and the position shows how and in what situations/life areas the behavior will play out.

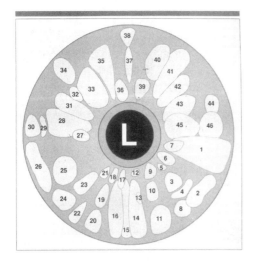 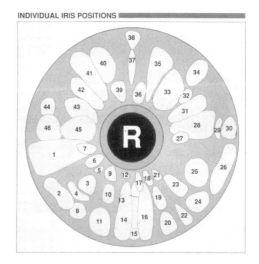

Diagrams courtesy of Rayid International, Mancos, Colorado

In Rayid, the bottom half of the iris has more of an impact on the personality than does the upper portion. One third of the bottom portion is associated with creativity and the emotions. Interestingly, the section of the iris farthest from the nose governs our social relations with others and how we express ourselves in groups. The medial region closest to the nose deals with our internal self and thoughts—habits and patterns that we may be unaware of. (Similarly, the lower portion of the astrological chart deals with the self and development of the personality, while the top portion deals with relationships to others and to the world.)

We can also see how the positions are related to the mental, emotional, and physical sections of the iris. Traits located closest to the pupil are more mental in nature and affect some aspect of the mind. Traits that fall in the midsection of the iris affect the person from an emotional standpoint. Traits in the outer portion of the iris are associated with the physical aspect of a person and their physical experiences.

A Rayid practitioner can determine the location and meaning of the various iris markings. There are 46 different positions in the iris, each relating to a certain attitude. Examples of some positions include the will, authority, nurturing, self-esteem, trust and achievement, competition, anger, jealousy versus sharing, achievement, patience, intimacy, pride, contemplation, understanding and compassion, relationships, our capacity for wisdom, and how we discriminate. Behavior is influenced by the characteristic associated with the area and the trait (Jewel, Flower, or Stream). Each trait in the iris is a gift that teaches us a lesson and helps us balance our personality.

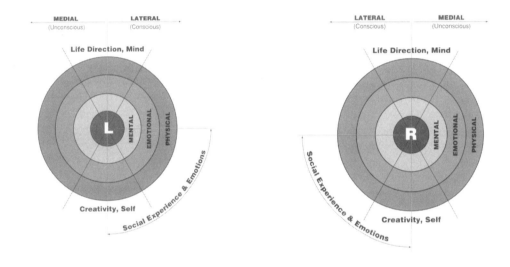

Diagrams courtesy of Rayid International, Mancos, Colorado

LEARNING FROM THE EYES

Experiencing people with different iris types allows us to learn, through observation, about the various qualities expressed in their irises, and about how these people think and approach life. We can then assimilate those qualities as we strive to become more complete. Rayid teaches us that there is often a strong attraction between opposite iris signs. The attraction, as in astrology, is partly due to the fact that our opposites possess the traits that are untapped within ourselves.

Through this process, we become more balanced. We feel less of a pull to other people. Relationships with others will no longer arise out of need and dependency; rather, they will provide other avenues for us to share, learn, and grow.

Opposites

To consciously live our wholeness, we must bring out and heal the parts of ourselves that we have repressed and kept hidden. Sometimes, these hidden parts reflect the qualities of our opposite, to which we are often attracted.

The Flower iris is emotional and expansive. Its opposite is the Jewel, which embodies the mental qualities and is more controlling and constricting. The Stream iris, calm and balanced, is in direct opposition to the Shaker, which swings from one extreme to the other, shaking up what is in balance. Even with similar core iris constitutions, there may be other opposite qualities that serve as attracting forces, such as introversion and extroversion. Our inner self knows we need to understand and develop some of these qualities, so we instinctively search for someone with those qualities. When we recognize this, we can learn from other people by observing their behavior.

Attraction can occur between opposites as well as between people with similar lessons. To heal ourselves, we seek someone with the greatest number of qualities that mirror the ones that we need to heal or develop within ourselves. Often, the more qualities someone has that we lack, the greater our attraction to that person. Relationships between opposites can be quite beautiful when the association is used to build and share understandings.

As we assimilate opposing qualities, we awaken to our wholeness. At first, we may feel "complete" when with our opposite, because they fill in what we lack. Unless we build independently the parts we lack, we can become dependent on our counterpart. Part of the healing process involves bringing out our dark side, or undeveloped or repressed characteristics.

Similars

When people of similar iris traits get together, they usually share mutual interests and have similar goals and ideals. Just like people with the same zodiac sign, they share a common bond because they understand each other at a deep level, similar to a brother-sister relationship. This type of relationship is healing because there is usually little or no conflict. Growth and learning come from the mirror effect: we reflect for each other the qualities we already possess.

TASKS

1. Obtain a complete Rayid iris analysis. See Rayid International's Web site for a list of certified practitioners: http://www.rayid.com.
2. Follow the recommendations made in your analysis for a month. Note differences in your mental, emotional, and physical health.
3. Frame and display photographs of your eyes as a reminder of your influences.

QUESTIONS

1. What is your core iris constitution? What are your strengths and weaknesses, gifts and talents?
2. What does your core iris constitution reveal about your life purpose?
3. What karmic lessons does your core iris constitution reveal?
4. Are you right- or left-brain dominant?
5. Are you introverted or extroverted?
6. Which iris rings have you identified?
7. In what ways does your job allow you to express your iris constitutional pattern?
8. In what way do your hobbies allow you to express your iris constitution?
9. In which area(s) of your life do you most easily reflect your core iris constitution?

EXERCISES

1. Trace your family ancestry to find the origin of some of your iris traits.
2. Identify all the strengths revealed in your iris. List ways you can incorporate them into your life.
3. Reflect on times when you were feeling great and in good health. At these times, to what extent were you using the gifts and talents revealed in your iris constitution?
4. Make a collage displaying your main iris characteristics. Incorporate images that you associate with each iris type.

5. List the choices you've made that were influenced by your iris pattern. De-
    scribe how these choices correspond to your iris pattern. For example, if you
    are a Stream and you chose to be a massage therapist, this choice reflects your
    desire to approach life kinesthetically.

[1] Denny Ray Johnson, *What the Eye Reveals* (Boulder, CO: Rayid Publications, 1995): 23

[2] Johnson, 9.

[3] Johnson, 55.

Six

Palmistry: Hands Hold the Answer

Giving Both Hands A Voice

My visit with a palm reader helped me change a lifelong pattern of indecisiveness and a belief that I would have to choose between a career and family. As the palm reader held my left hand she explained that my inner, emotional side was communicating to me to slow down, smell the roses, and enjoy life. It reflected my desire for nurturing relationships: this hand wanted to touch others and be a vehicle for giving and receiving love.

My right hand was communicating a different message. It wanted to be important in the world. This hand desired to write books, create, and invent. The message from this hand was to focus on my career above all. These different messages reflected the belief that I would have to give up one thing in order to have another.

The two hands also explained my vacillation in regard to intimate relationships. I often experienced doubt in committing to someone for fear that it might hinder my career ambitions.

This palm reading helped me see that both hands could work together. The key was to balance my time between relationships and career. Since making this shift in belief, I have formed a relationship with a man who has

also become my husband and business partner. He sup-
ports my goals and gives me the space I need to fulfill
them. This relationship has expanded both of our ca-
reers, enabling us to create more by combining our tal-
ents. The nurturing I receive from our relationship gives
me more energy to confront the challenges I encounter
at work. With both hands working cooperatively, I have
achieved an inner balance that allows me to touch more
lives through my creations.

This chapter explores the ancient science of palmistry. Palmistry is divided into two broad areas: the study of hand structure, known as cheirology, and the study of the palm lines, known as chiromancy. Our characteristics, traits, and behaviors reveal themselves in the shape, color, texture, and lines of our hands.

Palm reading has been associated with fortune-tellers for centuries in many cultures. The earliest book on palmistry, Hasta Samudrika Shastra (scriptures on the study of hands), was written in India in 3102 B.C.E. It is part of the sacred Vedas. The Chinese began hand reading 5,000 years ago to gain information about a person's health. Ancient Romans, Egyptians, Greeks (among them Aristotle and Hippocrates), and Hebrews acknowledged the significance of hands. They believed that certain areas of the hand relate to certain aspects of life, such as love, career, and creativity.

Hands reveal strengths, weaknesses, and karmic lessons. Like astrology and numerology, they show predominant personality traits and a person's potential. Every line also indicates something about how each area of life develops.

Palmists focus on several elements when reading hands. To see overall personality, they study:
1. Palm shape (disposition, mannerisms, temperament)
2. Finger shape and length (how we take action)
3. Fingerprints (past life challenges and life purpose)
4. Mounts (fleshy pads at the base of each finger). Each mount relates to the activities associated with a planet.
5. Life line (how we want to live life, our sexuality, sensuality and relationships)
6. Heart line (how we expresses emotions)
7. Head line (mental faculties)

8. Saturn line (security and foundations)
9. Mercury line (communication and our feelings of independence)

Other elements of the hand reveal more specific characteristics:
1. Color (health aspects of circulation and diet; general level of enthusiasm)
2. Muscle tone (energy level)
3. Skin texture (taste and style)
4. Flexibility (mental flexibility)
5. Markings on the lines and mounts (obstacles, energy flow, health, gifts and opportunities)

HAND TYPES

The first step in reading a hand is to note the shape of the palm. We can divide hands into two broad groups:
1. A square hand reflects a practical, down-to-earth person who needs stability. People with this palm shape are talented at working with their hands and have a high level of determination.
2. A rectangular hand reflects a more sensitive and intuitive person. Individuals with an oblong-shaped palm respond to life from a mental and emotional perspective.

When we combine the palm shape (temperament) with the finger length (how we take action), we find four hand types. Each type relates to one of the four elements: earth, air, water, and fire.
1. Earth hand (a square palm with short fingers): This type of hand belongs to a person who is organized, methodical, thorough, and competent. This practical person likes stability, finds it difficult to be spontaneous, and is a hard worker with a streak of impatience.
2. Air hand (fine skin texture, square palm with long fingers): Those who possess these hands respond to life from a mental and analytical perspective. They thrive on intellectual stimulation. These people are quick minded and adept communicators.
3. Water hand (graceful, with a rectangular-shaped palm and long fingers): People with these hands display remarkable intuitive and spiritual abilities. They have wonderful imaginations, which lends itself to extraordinary creativity. They are sensitive people who love beauty. Due to their emotional nature, they tend to be ungrounded and detached from the physical world

4. Fire hands (rectangular-shaped palm with short fingers): This type of hand belongs to action-oriented, energetic, and confident people. These extroverts possess an abundance of energy. Their charisma helps them rise to leadership positions.

Left and Right

The hand we write with—the sender, or active hand—is used to perform most mundane as well as creative tasks. This hand reveals our worldly ambitions and the part of ourselves that we present to the public. It is associated with the conscious mind and analytical abilities. The other hand—the receiver, or passive hand—represents the subconscious mind, our private self, imagination, emotions, and instinctual behaviors. We use this hand to support the writing hand. Ideally, we want to balance the sender and the receiver by using both parts of our mind. For example, when choosing a career (conscious mind), we can tap into our intuition (subconscious mind) to aid us in the decision-making process.

The dominant hand may also indicate which brain hemisphere we associate with more easily. Research has shown that the right- and left-brain hemispheres control functions of the opposite side of the body. The left hemisphere of the brain sends messages to the right hand, and vice versa. The left brain controls logical, rational thinking, while the right brain controls the imagination, emotions, intuition, and creativity. If the right hand is dominant, then the left brain is in charge of logical thinking. Hence, these folks usually respond more with their head than their heart. However, if the left hand is dominant, a switch occurs where the right side of the brain rules the logical thinking processes and the left hemisphere controls the emotions. This switch helps these people identify more with their heart.

Both hands must be examined and compared when doing a palm reading. Differences in the hands reflect a division between the inner and outer self, as you read in the story at the beginning of the chapter. Note the differences in lines, markings, mounts, and fingers.

CHARACTERISTICS

Hands

A reading begins with determining the gross characteristics of the hands relative to a person's height, weight, and other features.

- **Small and large:** Small hands indicate a person who views life on a grand scale, who prefers to focus on the big picture and avoid details. People with large hands tend to focus on details, often missing the big picture. They can be quite skilled as surgeons or jewelry makers due to their ability to concentrate.
- **Narrow and broad:** Narrow hands may belong to a person who is introverted and needs more time alone, whereas broad hands may reflect a more outgoing, practical person.
- **Thick and Thin:** Thick hands reflect a more energetic, extroverted, and sensual person, while thin hands reveal a more sensitive, reflective and introverted person.
- **Flexible and stiff:** The degree of flexibility in the hand and fingers reveals the flexibility in a person's thinking. A very flexible hand can bend back to a 90-degree angle. This person can roll with the punches. He loves freedom and challenges, and wants a career with opportunity for change. He sometimes has difficulty finishing projects. Stiff hands suggest a more cautious, stubborn person who has difficulty adapting to change; he tends to hold onto things. He wants stability in his career and other aspects of his life. He can be counted on to get things done.
- **Divisions of the hand:** Hands can be divided into conscious and subconscious zones. The conscious side concerns the areas of life you are aware of, such as your job and daily activities. The subconscious zone relates to more hidden motivations, the thoughts and feelings that often determine the actions you take on the conscious side.

Mounts

Both astrology and palmistry apply the qualities of the planets, which were named based on their affiliation with Greek and Roman gods to explain the influences that affect us. The palm of the hand is divided into five areas, each characterized by a specific energy (related to planetary characteristics) channeled through that area. For example, the area under the thumb is related to Venus, dealing with issues of love and beauty. The area under the middle finger is the Saturn area, dealing with issues of personal responsibility and maturity. To determine which mount is prominent, notice its size relative to the other mounts. Slightly cupping the hands will help you to determine the most significant mount.

Markings

Marks on the mounts will give you further information about that area of life. Note any of the following marks when reading the palm:

- **Squares:** a form of protection causing a person to get boxed in and stuck
- **Crosses and bars:** interaction and involvement with people
- **Triangles:** frustration and conflict
- **Grilles:** diffused and misdirected energy that causes us to waste time in activities not in alignment with our life purpose
- **Stars:** strong talents and abilities, usually developed in past lives. This effort leads to an intensification of energies, and possibly good fortune.

Following is a brief description of each mount. Note the similarities between these

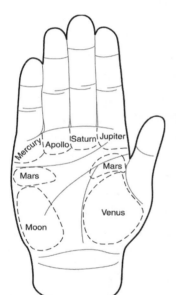

descriptions and those of the planets in astrology. An undeveloped mount indicates the lack of the qualities it normally represents. For example, a flat, colorless Venus mount would describe someone who lacks enjoyment and pleasure in life.

Jupiter (below the index finger): In mythology this god was generous and authoritative. This area is influenced by the qualities of expansion, charisma, ambition, law and order, justice, religion, and leadership. If the Jupiter mount predominates, we will have a sense of authority, confidence, and leadership skills.

Saturn (below the middle finger): This god was associated with duty, responsibility, and was, therefore, quite serious. This influence helps us to face our duties and mature. People with prominent Saturn mounts are usually self-disciplined, conservative, industrious, skeptical, and prefer solitude. They would do well to learn generosity.

Sun (below the ring finger): The Sun is associated with self-expression. This area reveals our potential for success in creative endeavors. It is easy to spot people with a pronounced Sun mount because they are happy, optimistic, and friendly. They also attract attention due to their flashy style.

Mercury (below the pinkie finger): Mercury, messenger of the gods, deals with communication, mental abilities, and written and verbal skills. People with a predominant Mount of Mercury are usually good at learning languages, writing, and business due to their quick mind. Mercury people are multitalented and will do well in a profession where they can apply their mental abilities and diplomatic skills.

Venus (at the ball of the thumb): Venus deals with beauty of all kinds, love, passion, and compassion. Individuals with a strong Venus mount will exude good health, warmth, and compassion. They enjoy the senses and the beautiful things in life. Their aesthetic nature is revealed in their surroundings.

Mars (two locations: outer border where the Mount of Mercury borders the heart line, and between Jupiter and Venus): The middle of the hand area is called the plain of Mars. Mars energy is powerful and aggressive, reflecting the qualities of the god of war. People with a pronounced Mount of Mars use these qualities to take initiative: they are determined, forceful, and courageous. They know how to overcome obstacles.

Moon (the side of the hand beneath the little finger, beginning below the Mount of Mercury): This area is concerned with emotions, intuition, and imagination. People with a predominant Moon Mount may channel their imagination into writing, music, or other artistic avenues. They need to be careful not to live in the clouds and separate themselves from reality. Moon people are idealistic, sensitive, and intuitive. They are flexible and want to nurture others.

Fingers

Fingers offer even more specific information about personality. They reveal how we use our talents. Each finger corresponds to the mount below it. For example, the index finger is known as the Jupiter finger. The longer and bigger the finger relative to the length of the palm, the greater the degree to which the person will take on the Jupiter qualities. A palm reading may include examination of fingernails, fingertips, and fingerprints.

Short and long: We begin with an assessment of finger length. Use the middle Saturn finger as your guide. If this finger is about as long as your palm (seven-eighths of an inch) it is considered long. Long fingers indicate a more intellectual, patient person, who likes details and has difficulty seeing the big picture. If the finger is shorter than seven-eighths of the length of the palm it is considered short.

Short fingers represent an impulsive, impatient nature. People with short fingers see the whole picture and often overlook details.

Flexibility: Flexibility reveals the ability to be versatile with our talents. The more flexible the fingers, the easier a person can express and apply his talents in diverse ways.

Thin and thick: Thin fingers reflect a person who is intellectual; thick fingers indicate those who are earthy and more sensual.

Knuckles: Smooth knuckles belong to people who apply their talents quickly and spontaneously. Knotty fingers reflect analytical people who spend more time deciding how they will apply their gifts and talents.

Jupiter (index finger): This finger deals with ambition, leadership potential and our spiritual nature. This is the finger that we point with, hence it reflects our assertiveness. A person with a long finger is very ambitious, and may be bossy. The shorter finger indicates that a person may suffer from self-doubt.

Saturn (middle finger): This finger reveals how you deal with responsibility. A long finger shows you strongly identify with the Saturn qualities of seriousness and productivity, while a shorter finger indicates a lack of these qualities.

Sun (ring finger): A long finger endows a person with creative talent. Such people are risk takers and run with their ideas. A shorter finger indicates a more practical person who acts prudently and wants guarantees before taking action.

Mercury (pinkie finger): This finger is associated with all forms of communication. A long finger indicates someone with good communication skills, while a short finger narrows the self- expression.

Thumb: Thumbs represent our will and ability to assert ourselves. They represent how well we can manifest our goals and desires and to what degree we can influence our surroundings. Long thumbs offer the potential to develop great willpower. Those with short thumbs may have to work harder to develop their will, although they are stable and very responsible.

Finger Tips
The tips offer further information about how we channel our energy and talents to the world. Fingers may not all share the same shape, so each must be evaluated separately.

- Square tip: practical, structured, meticulous
- Spatulate tip: action oriented, dynamic thinkers and innovators, they change and break rules and tradition
- Pointed tip: sensitive, intuitive, impractical
- Round tip: social people who love variety and dispersing knowledge

Finger Spacing

Put your hand on a table or up in the air and notice the spacing of the fingers. When all the fingers have spaces between them, it indicates you are using your talents and abilities. Fingers held tightly together indicate that a person is restricting the expression of his talents. A thumb held close to the hand reveals a more closed, inhibited person who moves with caution. He may have difficulty influencing his surroundings. A thumb held open at a 45–90-degree angle reveals a more open, relaxed person. These people are more confident due to their ability to shape their environment according to their needs.

LINES

The type and position of each line reveals something about the flow of energy to the area of life represented in that section of the palm. They reveal the past and possible future events. They can depict our state of health, mental and emotional tendencies, creative abilities, relationships, travel opportunities, intuitive abilities, and the degree to which we are fulfilling our life purpose. The deeper the line, the stronger its influence. Many lines indicate that a person has many interests and will explore many paths in life. Sensitivity increases with the number of lines. A hand with fewer lines decreases the sensitivity and indicates fewer avenues for life expression.

Lines are formed when a child is in the womb and may change as the child grows. The shape of the lines will not usually change, however, they may grow branches or become deeper or fainter in response to changes in thoughts. Due to the relationship between the nervous system and the hands, a line is imprinted on the hands when signals from the nervous system are sent.

Markings

In addition to the marks that can be found on the mounts, the following patterns can influence the activity of the line:
- Dots: a physical or emotional trauma or setback
- Breaks/splits: a change of direction

- Splinters: a dissipation of focus and strength
- Islands: stagnation
- Chain (a string of islands): a prolonged period of weakness and scattered energy
- Branches: movement or focus in a particular direction, depending on where it points. Branches that rise upwards are a positive influence; those that point downward represent a setback, which takes away from the power of the line.
- Forks: an increase in the line energy, with the exception of the placement on the life line, which dissipates physical stamina and resistance.

Palmists examine several significant lines during a reading, including some secondary lines not mentioned in this book. When we examine a line, we look at its depth and clarity, shape, length, start and finish positions, its relationship to other lines, and markings.

Life or Earth Line

Reading from the top down, the line (corresponding to the early years in life) begins at the area below the index finger and moves down towards the wrist along the ball of the thumb. Contrary to popular belief, the life line does not reveal our length of life; rather, it shows how we live our life, our sensuality and sexuality, relationships, and overall health. The Chinese refer to it as the major earth line, since it describes our physical expression.

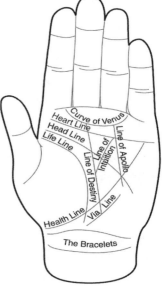

- Clarity: A strong line reflects a strong constitution, and a weaker line decreases the vitality.
- Shape: A curved line that stretches far away from the thumb reveals an open and generous person. If the line hugs the thumb, the person will be more closed and introverted.
- Length: Long: great stamina. Short: A person often makes major life changes, reflecting her desire for freedom.
- Start and Finish: If it ends under the ball of the thumb in the mount of Venus area, the person loves to be with family. If it ends more towards the middle of the palm, the person will be more interested in traveling and moving away from family.
- Line Relationships: When the line connects to the head line, the person will be more cautious, taking time to make decisions. The longer the two lines

are connected, the longer he will reflect before making a decision. A life line that does not touch the head line reflects someone who is more impatient and extroverted.

Heart Line

The heart line is the line closest to the mounts. It reveals information about our emotional nature and the ability to express our feelings.

- Clarity: Strong: A warm, caring person who freely expresses feelings. Weak: This person has more of a tendency to repress his emotional energy.
- Shape: A curved line reflects a more passionate, feeling-oriented person who needs to express his emotions. A straight line reveals someone with a more cautious and reserved approach to love who allows his head to rule his heart. A fork at the end indicates a balance among sexuality, emotion, and intellect.
- Length: Long, ending under the Jupiter finger: Harmonious relationships are important for these people, who easily share their love with others. They are receptive to others' emotions and enjoy helping other people. Peace and harmony are their goals. Short, ending under the Saturn finger: These people will be more protective of their emotions and generally less expressive. They may prefer to devote more time to work than to relationships.
- Start and Finish: A line that ends between Saturn and Jupiter brings balance between the head and heart.
- Line Relationships: A wide space between the heart and head lines creates openness and a desire for interaction with others. A narrow space between these two lines creates more introversion and narrow-mindedness.

Head Line

Starting near or at the same point as the life line, the head line reveals how we reason, use our intellect, and process information. The Chinese refer to this line as the air line. This line offers valuable information about a person's memory and ability to concentrate. It may also reveal periods of emotional difficulty and mental illness.

- Clarity: Strong: A focused mind capable of long periods of concentration. Weak: An undisciplined mind that has difficulty with concentration and decision making.
- Shape: A straight line reveals a practical, analytical thinker. A curved line signals a more creative and imaginative thinker. A wavy line reflects vacillation.
- Length: Long (reaching under the Mercury finger): Someone who is multitalented and has many interests and a curious mind. Short (reaching the Saturn finger): The person is more concerned with mundane affairs and the

practical application of information. She prefers to focus on one area rather than diversify.

- Start and Finish: A slight curve downward creates a balance between logic and imagination. A large curve down into the Moon area indicates a highly imaginative person who can easily tap into her intuition.
- Relation to other lines: If the head line blends with the heart line, it creates an intense expression. When they blend into one line it is called a Simian line.

Saturn Line

Also referred to as the destiny line, fate line, or minor earth line in the Chinese system, this line begins at the bottom of the hand and usually moves upward toward the Saturn mount. The line deals with issues of survival, security, and the ability to build a foundation. It indicates the degree of ambition directed toward one's goals.

- Clarity: Strong: An ambitious, secure person who is self-directed and knows what he wants. She is capable of building a solid foundation for herself and meeting her needs.
- Weak: He may be insecure and lack the motivation to direct himself. He needs to ground himself and set goals.
- Non-existent: People who do not have this line tend to be rebels who pave their own path. They may reject all responsibilities and duties.
- Length: Long: She may remain active past the retirement age, always busy pursuing goals. Short: She may not work during her later years, or will tend to stick with the career and goals she formed earlier in life.
- Start and Finish: The farther up on the hand this line begins, the later in life he will find security and a sense of purpose. Lines starting on the Mount of the Moon bring the element of creativity into the career. Lines beginning on the inside of the life line indicate that the family will have a strong influence on her career choices. Lines ending on the Jupiter mount enhance her chances of attaining positions of leadership and influence. A line ending between the Saturn and the Sun fingers indicates a career in the arts. The most common ending position is under Saturn, which highlights a responsible and serious nature. A double Saturn line may indicate a plurality of goals and possibly more than one occupation.

Mercury Line

Also known as the hepatica or health line, the Mercury line runs diagonally from the life line towards the Mount of Mercury. Although not present in all hands, those that have this line are endowed with creativity and good communication skills. A strong line reveals someone who is independent and opinionated.

Curve of Venus

A semicircular line located between the heart line and the top of the palm, the curve of Venus is also referred to as the line of Neptune because of its association with the emotions. People with this line possess sensitivity and compassion. They need to bring out their emotions in a humanitarian way. This influence brings added empathy to a person who may tend to take things personally.

Special Markings

Spiritual aspects found on the hand are important to understanding our life purpose. The degree to which we have focused on our spiritual development in past and present lives is evidenced by several marks.

- Moon Line: This is a curved line that forms a half circle on the Moon Mount. Individuals with this line can see beyond the physical world. They are the clairvoyants and psychics.
- Lines of Jupiter: These are short, vertical lines found on the Mount of Jupiter just below the finger. They indicate an interest in spiritual subjects.

MOON AND JUPITER LINE

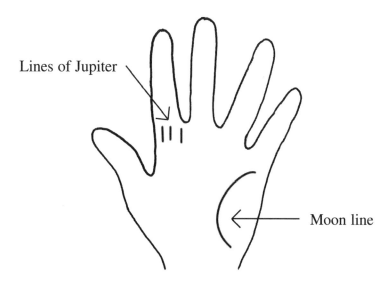

LIFE LINE

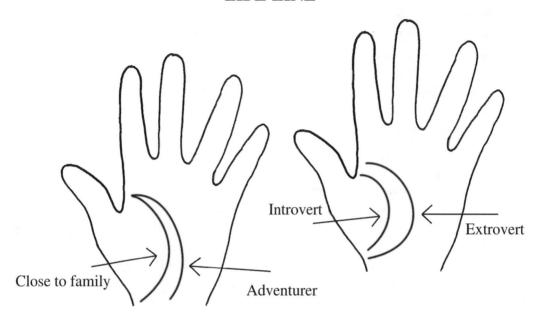

Introvert

Extrovert

Close to family

Adventurer

HEART LINE

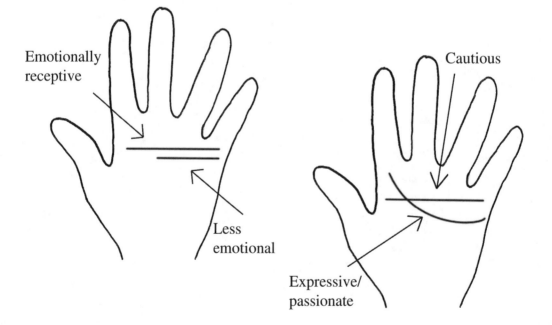

Emotionally
receptive

Cautious

Less
emotional

Expressive/
passionate

HEAD LINE

MERCURY LINE

SATURN LINE

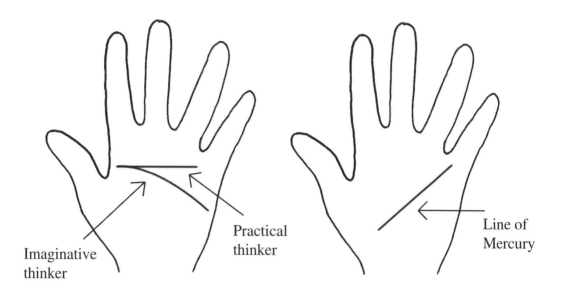

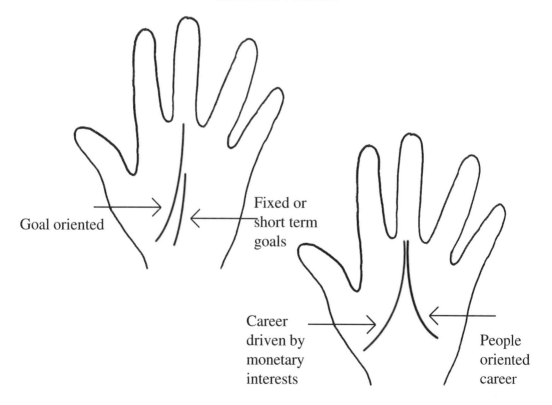

Practical thinker

Imaginative thinker

Line of Mercury

Goal oriented

Fixed or short term goals

Career driven by monetary interests

People oriented career

MARKINGS

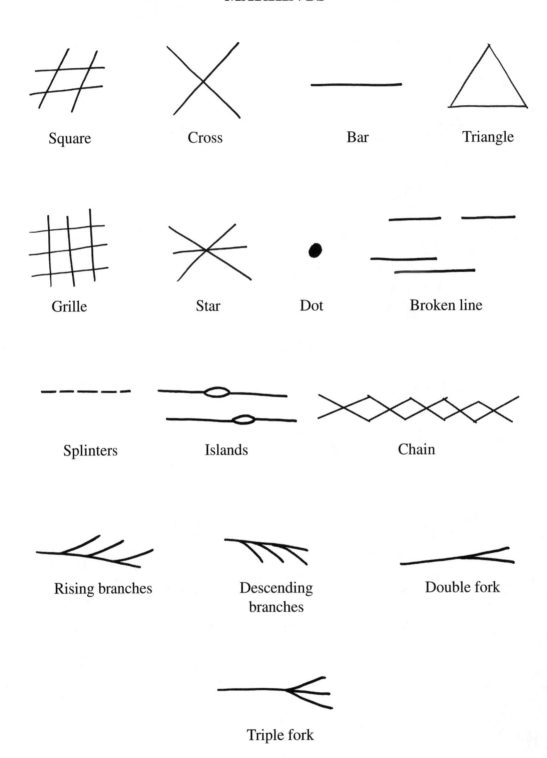

Square   Cross   Bar   Triangle

Grille   Star   Dot   Broken line

Splinters   Islands   Chain

Rising branches   Descending branches   Double fork

Triple fork

READ YOUR PALMS

Use the following Hand Analysis Chart to read your palms. If you'd like a visual reminder of your influences and soul choices, you may have photographs taken of your palms. For a less expensive process, follow the instructions on making handprints in the Tasks section.

When you consult a palmist, refer to this chapter to ensure that you receive a complete reading. Remember that hands offer guidance, revealing only potential and possibilities: we have the power to shape our own destiny.

HAND ANALYSIS CHART

Hands

Palm Shape (square, rectangular):

Finger length (long, short):

Type (earth, fire, air, water):

Size (large, small, narrow, broad):

Flexibility (flexible, stiff):

Thin / thick:

Mounts

Strongest:

Weakest:

Markings:

Fingers

Flexibility:

Length (short, long):

Thick/thin:

Smooth or knotty knuckles:

Fingers and fingertips:

Jupiter:

Saturn:

Sun:

Mercury:

Thumb:

Predominant finger:

Finger spacing:

Lines (depth and clarity, shape, length, start and finish positions, relationship to other lines, special markings)

Life:

Heart:

Head:

Saturn:

Mercury:

Curve of Venus:

Strongest line:

Spiritual Marks
Moon Line:

Lines of Jupiter:

Comparison of right and left hand (Note major differences between the hands.):

Hand Analysis Summary:

TASKS

Obtain a palm reading. I recommend contacting Vernon Mahabal at the Palmistry Institute for a trained palmist. He may be reached at 1-866-269-7256 (PALM) or at palmistryinstitute@yahoo.com. You may also check his Web site: www.palmistryinstitute.com. Vernon is available for readings and workshops.

1. Create your handprints. **Materials:** 1 rubber roller (about 4 inches wide); 1 tube black, water-based block printing ink; art paper; 1 pad foam rubber; material to apply the ink, such as newspaper or a flat piece of glass or acrylic. **Steps:** Place a sheet of art paper on foam rubber. Roll ink onto the glass or newspaper. Apply the inked roller to the palm only. Use ink sparingly. Place the hand on the art paper. Press to make a deep impression. Remove hand slowly, holding the paper down to avoid smudges.
2. Identify the most prominent mount. Then read the characteristics of the planet associated with that mount.
3. Compare the right and left hands. List the differences between the two.

EXERCISES

1. List the challenging and favorable aspects shown on your palms. Write a plan describing how you will overcome the challenges and use the favorable qualities to the fullest.
2. Write about how you have used your hands to fulfill your life purpose.
3. Write a poem about your hands. Include what you learned from the reading you received.
4. Briskly rub your hands together for a minute and slowly separate them. Feel the energy flow between them.

QUESTIONS

1. How have your hands served you throughout your life?
2. List any preconceived ideas you had about palmists. Describe how these ideas have changed after reading this book.

Seven

Family: Our Spiritual Heritage

Different Roles, Similar Lessons

While hearing about a past life my family spent together (in Australia in the 1830s), I realized that, although our roles were different then, we behave in similar patterns.

Dad expects Mom to be housewife and mother; Mom expects Dad to provide for the family. When either does not live up to expectations, difficulties arise. The past life report taught them that, to keep love flowering, they needed to create together.

In the past lifetime, my father and sister were husband and wife, in a union soured by abuse and conflict. They are still trying to overcome the tendency to judge and criticize each other. At times, my father's judgments cause my sister to reject him. The past life report helped them see the need to express love for each other. As they suspend judgment, they work toward greater understanding and acceptance of each other.

In both lifetimes, I envied my sister, her wonderful home life, marriage, children, and lovely house. My sister wished for more time for a career and spiritual studies, areas on which I've focused. The report helped us realize that we provide great stimulus for each other to get in touch with our own desires. My sister has since made time for spiritual pursuits by reading books and join-

ing me on several spiritual retreat weekends. I have created more balance in my life by devoting more time to relationships.

My mother and sister, twin sisters in the past, share many of the same traits and interests as they did then. They both love interior decorating and enjoy devoting time to their families. When they are creating something together, they form a dynamic team. However, they experience friction when one exhibits an unproductive quality such as fear. The past life report helped them discover the source of their reactions. Their similarities, mirrors for each other, help them learn more about both positive and negative qualities. Now, when one recognizes a bothersome trait in the other, she looks within to see what is being mirrored. As a result, my sister has faced her biggest fear: completing a course to become a professional decorator. Mom has encouraged her all the way.

The lesson? Love comes from creating together, from making plans and dreaming together, and is squashed by judgments, expectations, and imposing role stereotypes. Our family can grow and evolve by letting go of expectations and judgments. With practice, we have opened ourselves up to the feelings and thoughts that we provoke in each other.

THE SOUL'S CHOICE

The family unit is a complex mixture of personalities who come together to learn, heal, and love. It is the first place we begin our Earthly journey. Even before our soul enters the physical body, we are receptive to the thoughts and feelings of the mother we chose.

A soul chooses the period, country, gender, and family into which it incarnates, seeking the greatest learning opportunities based on its needs. The family is the most significant of these choices. Family is instrumental in helping us fulfill our soul's purpose by helping us learn karmic lessons and providing an environment in which we can develop our gifts and talents. Even dysfunctional families offer the appropriate lessons. When we accept responsibility for such choices, we see why we chose our parents.

Our family plays a significant part in the development of our beliefs and attitudes about the world. Most of our beliefs about the world are formed by the age of seven. Before this age, children absorb the thoughts and attitudes of the people around them. If we are to understand ourselves, we must understand our family.

KARMA AND FAMILY

When we understand our family dynamics, we understand our karmic destiny. Have you ever heard anyone remark, "I feel as though I've married my mother (or father)"? If we don't master the lessons offered by our family members, we find people later in life who mirror our parents, giving us another chance to learn the lesson. Delving into family memories can sometimes be painful, frightening, or pleasantly nostalgic. Volatile emotions signal the need to understand family karma. When we can objectively view family members, our relationship to them, and our childhood without pain or charged emotion, we will have taken a major step toward clearing family karma.

Each of us has individual karma. Families have collective or group karma. All family members learn from each other. Thus, the family unit transforms itself into a melting pot of individual and shared lessons. When the members are conscious and communicate openly, the potential for growth and transcendent love is heightened.

Souls also unite within a family to fulfill a common purpose. Many families unite to create something such as a family business, or work together as volunteers for a charitable organization. Creation is a spiritual act; families that engage in a common creative project usually grow closer.

Family is the first place we learn about giving and receiving; as children, we are usually receiving. While raising children, parents learn unconditional love and how to put others' needs before their own. Parents learn to listen to their children, physically and intuitively. Before children learn to speak, parents must "tune in" to recognize their needs and thoughts. Most parents agree that they receive so much pleasure from watching their children grow and learn that personal sacrifices seem insignificant.

BELIEFS

Our belief system, shaped mainly by our family, serves as the basis for many of our choices. Consciously and unconsciously, we allow beliefs to imbed themselves in our mind. Limiting beliefs such as "money doesn't grow on trees" and "children should be seen but not heard" can greatly limit the expression of our life purpose. Answer the questions at the end of this chapter to uncover your hidden beliefs.

SIMILARITIES AND DIFFERENCES

The similar traits and beliefs that our parents shared are most likely the things we have easily integrated into ourselves. Make a list of their similar qualities, then notice which ones you have developed within yourself. Take it a step further and separate them into positive and negative columns.

The differences between your parents may signal areas where you need to find balance within yourself. Put your mother's qualities in one column and your father's in another. If you realize one parent was overly serious while the other was more carefree, look within yourself to see how you vacillate between these two qualities. Then, find a balance between the two or choose one quality over the other.

Similarities between Parents

1.

2.

3.

Differences between Parents

Mother	Father
1.	1.
2.	2.
3.	3.

Beliefs Learned from Parents

1.

2.

3.

ANCESTORS

Ancestors and siblings also play a part in understanding the dynamics. Heredity stretches beyond physical traits such as eye and skin color to encompass patterns of thinking: we also inherit the thoughts and attitudes of our parents and other ancestors. The more we become aware of these transgenerational patterns, the less we act out the unconscious behaviors of our ancestors. We must look at the entire family tree—not only our parents—to trace the origin of many of our traits.

Each one of us is capable of changing family beliefs and attitudes. By taking responsibility for changing outdated and limiting belief patterns, we can pave a more expansive path for future generations to attain greater prosperity. The progress made by one person will affect everyone else. As with other methods of self-awareness, the study of family is not meant to place blame for negative traits. It is, rather, a self-empowerment tool to eliminate what is unproductive and to develop gifts and talents.

BIRTH ORDER

Denny Johnson, originator of the Rayid method, discovered universal traits, common to people born in a particular birth order, that shape their personality. His research, outlined in *The Nature of Birth Order,* also sheds light on issues of sibling rivalry and parent-child relationships.

Sibling Sequence

There are twelve basic patterns in birth order, each represented by a "brother" or "sister." Each sibling type embodies a unique set of traits and learning. Together, they represent all the masculine and feminine qualities. By assimilating all these character traits, we can diversify and access more of our wisdom. We can also develop greater love for ourselves and for our brothers and sisters.

The father determines birth order; the number of children a mother has is irrelevant. If a man has two sons with his first wife, another son with a second wife would be considered boy number 3. A child that survives after 16 weeks of gestation is considered part of the birth order sequence, even if the baby dies before birth. After child number 6, the next child would begin the sequence again at number one, taking on the qualities of a firstborn. The eighth child would possess the qualities of a number 2 sibling, and so on. Being born after a member of the opposite sex will also modify characteristics: the first-born determines the gender sequence. For example, a third-born girl born after two boys will possess the qualities of a third boy, expressed in a more feminine way, as well as a number 1 girl. A firstborn son born after two girls would take on the qualities of the firstborn son, as well as those of a third-born girl, in a more masculine way. A second-born girl born after a boy will be a mixture of the competitive, aggressive, and ambitious traits of boy number 2, and the organized, controlling "queen" of the household disposition of girl number 1.

As you read the descriptions of each sibling, keep in mind that the characteristics of each child will be modified by the birth order of parents and grandparents. For example, a child raised by a mother who was the firstborn girl will be influenced differently than if she were the fourth-born child. In addition, divorce, adoptions, death, and social influences all create dynamics that can modify the birth order traits.

Let's look at the qualities of the six boys and six girls in terms of their karmic lessons, inherent nature, and gifts. As you read these descriptions, keep in mind the following patterns. Lessons of the yang siblings are to learn to use power correctly. Lessons of the yin siblings are to be more open and receptive. The yin siblings are from the mother's side of the family, while the yang siblings are from the father's side.

1. Boys with birth order numbers 2, 4, and 6 are emotionally oriented, extroverted, and express the yang energy predominantly.
2. Boys with birth order numbers 1, 3, and 5 are more mentally oriented, introverted, and express more yin energy.
3. Girls with birth order numbers 2, 4, and 6 are more yin in nature and feeling oriented.
4. Girls with birth order numbers 1, 3, and 5 possess more of the yang energy, and are more mentally oriented.

BOYS

Birth Order	Gifts	Lessons
1	independent, mechanically dexterous, inventive mind; creative and gentle; introverted, can become a good leader and visionary	humility, peace
2	determined, aggressive, competitive, intense, good motor skills, athletic; good at setting and fulfilling goals; if focused can become a champion in any area	self-discipline, emotional control, find purpose, build self-respect
3	clever, ease in talking, diplomatic, powerful mental capabilities, good concentration, good at networking, playful, can be good strategist and negotiator	express himself honestly, increase self-awareness
4	sharp mind, helpful, skilled at integrating and synthesizing information; humorous and charismatic; can capture people's attention	loyalty, develop alliances, a sense of kinship and playfulness
5	believes in fairness and justice, dislikes conflict; wants to serve others; gentle, kind; brings peace and tenderness to any activity	focus, express himself, develop creativity and independence
6	practical visionary with power to change the world; revolutionary who is good at using and directing his power; alert, dynamic, domineering; a natural leader in politics or other arenas	tolerance, direction, control of the will, build leadership skills, correct use of power

GIRLS

Birth Order	Gifts	Lessons
1	strong, practical; mission is to heal the family; likes to control; great teacher, loyal family member	concentrate, be responsible and maintain playfulness
2	mysterious, subtle, cool, expressive, determined, artistic, sharp mind, vivid imagination, successful at creative endeavors and business ventures	communicate thoughts, peace, emotional control
3	cooperative; yearns for equality and fairness; gentle, sensitive, good facilitator; often does community service; earthy; can use understanding of harmony and love in teaching, meditation and healing professions	blend fairness and firmness to bring justice, develop personal stability
4	a revolutionary; may seek to better humanity through radical behavior; inspired, futuristic thinking can be channeled into teaching or philosophy	receive without judgment, forgive and release
5	caring, nurturing, humble, sensitive; brings peace and community, excels in positions of service; shows compassion for all living things because she recognizes her connection to everything	expand vision and love to all humanity
6	sweet, intelligent, creative, visionary, loves humanity; often drawn to religious or spiritual life	develop spirituality through silence, purifying intentions

GRANDPARENTS

Grandparents play a special role in family dynamics. Although we may spend less time with them than we do with our parents, they are important influences. Johnson found that, based on birth order, each sibling has a special connection with a particular grandparent, demonstrated by the many traits and attitudes that sibling inherits. Check the following chart to find the ancestor that holds the most powerful key to understanding yourself.

BOYS		GIRLS	
Birth Order	**Grandparent**	**Birth Order**	**Grandparent**
1	maternal grandfather	1	paternal grandmother
2	paternal grandfather	2	maternal grandmother
3	mother's maternal grandfather	3	father's paternal grandmother
4	father's paternal grandfather	4	mother's maternal grandmother
5	mother's paternal grandfather	5	father's maternal grandmother
6	father's maternal grandfather	6	mother's paternal grandmother

The questions at the end of the chapter will help you better understand the influence your mother and father had on you. What did you learn from each of them? Notice how you related to them. (To open the subconscious mind, create a journal about your parents. Through writing, you will express many hidden thoughts otherwise not revealed.)

Did your mother or your father dominate? What patterns existed? Was there alcoholism, verbal or physical abuse, neglect, divorce, incest, lying, infidelity, or other dysfunctional pattern? Identify positive patterns, such as sharing, unconditional love, concern, and hard work. Before you do the tasks, questions, and exercises, say a prayer of gratitude to your parents for the lessons they gave you. When you release negativity towards your family, you will be more open to the insights awaiting you.

Despite arguments and disagreements, we know that our family members will not usually abandon us. An open, accepting environment is vital because mastering karmic lessons often comes after long periods of conflict and disagreement. Families willing to risk expressing themselves, work through conflicts, and remain together can achieve tremendous growth. Family members who support and encourage each other's talents help a soul fulfill its purpose. Below is a story of how one family's love and encouragement led to one of the greatest musical talents in history.

A Perfect Choice of Parents

Born on January 27, 1756 to Leopold and Anna Maria Mozart in the town of Salzburg, Austria, Wolfgang chose the perfect family. Leopold was a violinist and music teacher, the ideal father to encourage Wolfgang to pursue his musical interests. As a child, Wolfgang would go to sleep listening to his father and sister play music. His early exposure to music inspired him to teach himself to play the clavier at the age of three. After much pleading, Leopold agreed to give his son music lessons a year later. Soon thereafter, his father helped him compose his first song by writing down the notes as he played.

A loving and supportive father, Leopold also became Wolfgang's teacher and manager. When he recognized his son's potential, he took time off from his job to teach and promote him, arranging tours and performances throughout Europe.

Leopold's struggles with money proved to also be a karmic lesson for Wolfgang. Despite attempts to earn more money and advance his musical career, Leopold was unsuccessful. His hope that Wolfgang would attain more financial success never materialized. He managed his money poorly. He did not learn from his father's money problems, and died in poverty.

Wolfgang Amadeus Mozart composed 22 operas, 48 symphonies, 25 piano concertos, 15 masses, and more than a dozen shorter religious compositions. His loving father remained his most devoted supporter and died only four years before his son.

TASKS

1. Write a letter to each person in your family thanking them for what they taught you.
2. Obtain a family past life reading (a collective report of up to five family members).
3. Do a past life regression based on your family.
4. Plan a family event or trip deviating from your usual routines. What did you discover about each family member in this new environment?
5. Create a family tree. Indicate the most outstanding trait you learned from each person. Identify where you learned some of your beliefs and behaviors.
6. List the lessons, gifts, and talents of your birth order position.
7. Write a mythological story about how your family came together.
8. Write a story with your children about a past life you think you shared.
9. Create something—a photo album, a garden, a meal—as a family unit. Creating unites souls in a common endeavor.
10. Write about your childhood memories including what you imagined or fantasized about, the activities you enjoyed and the careers you wanted to pursue.

QUESTIONS

1. What were your mother's strengths and weaknesses? Your father's?
2. What is the most important thing you learned from your mother? From your father?
3. What did you learn from your mother about women and femininity? From your father about men and masculinity?
4. What do you admire most about the relationship between your parents?
5. Who played the dominant role in the household?
6. How do you feel about authority figures? What role did your parents play in contributing to these feelings?
7. Describe how your past and current intimate relationships parallel your parents' relationship. How do they differ?
8. How do (did) your mother and father view themselves? Be sure to include their level of self-esteem. Describe any similarities with how you view yourself.
9. Describe family communication. Was it superficial? Were you able to share deep thoughts and feelings?
10. What was the work ethic in your family?
11. What was the role of religion in your family?
12. Describe any favoritism toward siblings. Did you receive enough attention growing up? Explain.

13. What did you like best about your family? Least?
14. What did you imagine or fantasize about as a child?
15. What activities stimulated your curiosity as a child?
16. What careers did you want to follow as a child?
17. What beliefs did you learn from your parents?

EXERCISES

1. Starting with your earliest memories, describe your childhood, until puberty, with your mother. What was she like in the areas of affection, discipline, teaching, religion, social life, work, and your puberty? Be as specific as possible. Write without stopping in a stream-of-consciousness manner.
2. Do the same exercise for your father.
3. List the karmic lessons that exist between you and each member of your family.
4. List the gifts and talents that you learned from family members or that they helped you cultivate.
5. Based on the answers to exercises 3 and 4, write the reasons you chose your family.
6. Ask your mother and father to tell you stories about your childhood. Compare their memories to your own. Note any significant differences.
7. Do some psychodrama (dramatization) activities of family events. For example, replay a typical family dinner at your house with friends or relatives. Describe the personalities of each family member to your friends so they can accurately play the roles. This exercise gives you the opportunity to objectively observe your role and the way you interacted with others in the family. Describe your discoveries.
8. Which family members' thoughts can you pick up on intuitively? Describe the situations where you intuitively knew what that family member was thinking.

Eight

Assembling the Pieces:
The Puzzle Takes Form

During the first part of the journey to finding a life purpose, we have been seekers gathering all the pieces of the puzzle. The next part of the journey will entail sorting the pieces and putting them together. The closer the puzzle gets to completion, the closer we get to discovering our life purpose. The case study at the end of this chapter illustrates one person's assembled puzzle.

Our astrological profile reveals a part of who we are. We also have qualities and talents that were built in past lives. Vibrational eye patterns and numerology reports contribute even more dimensions to unveiling our personality. This chapter explores how the information from all the approaches to self-awareness we've touched on blend together. We will look for karmic lessons, strengths, and weaknesses that are enhanced and/or diminished by certain influences as well as for lessons and talents that appear more than once, either within one approach of self-awareness or independently in two different approaches.

Many influences within each approach work together to create personal balance. For example, Rayid iris may show a Jewel constitution with right-brain dominance. The Jewel influence portrays the ability to reason logically; right-brain dominance helps bring out creativity and flexibility.

Influences of more than one approach may create balance as well. An astrological chart may show a majority of air signs, describing a highly intellectual, logical thinker. The iris may show a Flower pattern, which expresses life through the emotions and adds creativity to the personality. The Flower pattern balances the dominant air sign activity so the individual will not be too analytical or out of touch with his or her emotions. Together, the two influences balance the person.

COMPARING THE METHODS

In chapter one I described the various ways in which each method of self-awareness is connected. Now that you have a broader understanding of each method we can take a closer look at the similarities between them. This will aid us to see how all these influences blend together. We can then look at our own reports and determine how to best work with all our influences.

Rayid Iris and Astrology

The four main iris structures in Rayid; Jewel, Flower, Stream, Shaker, have similarities with the four elements in astrology, air, earth, fire and water.

- The Jewel is similar to the air signs Gemini, Libra, and Aquarius. People with these influences experience and respond to life through the mind and the intellect.

- The Flower is similar to the earth signs Taurus, Virgo and Capricorn. The common urge with these influences is to create in all forms.

- The Stream is similar to the water signs Pisces, Cancer and Scorpio. Streams and water signs are fluid, sensitive and caring people. They nurture and connect with people on an emotional level.

- The Shaker is similar to the fire signs Leo, Sagittarius and Aries. People with these influences have a dynamic zest for life, and they take action to bring forth revolutionary change.

The core iris constitution is equivalent to the sun sign. Both of these will have the most significant impact on an individual's personality and life direction. The iris rings modify the core iris constitution in the same way that the Ascendant and placement of the 10 planets affect a person's sun sign. Both the iris and an astrology chart are maps, which can be divided up into different areas of life. The location of traits within the iris and the location of planets within the 12 houses indicate how a particular trait will affect a person.

Rayid Iris and Numerology

Each iris constitution has a similar vibration to the numbers 1-9, 11 and 22. Below are the examples.

- Jewel: 1, 4 and 7. The Jewel possesses the leadership qualities of the 1, the stability of the 4, and the mental acumen of the 7.

- Flower: 3, 5 and 22. The Flower possesses the charisma, enthusiasm and the desire for self-expression of the 3, combined with the adaptability and the adventuresome spirit of the 5. Similar to the 22, they can channel their creative visions into reality.

- Stream: 6, 2 and 11. The Stream shares the caring and nurturing qualities of the 6, the desire for peace, harmony and relationships of the 2, and the intuitive skills of the 11.

- Shaker: 8 and 9. The Shaker, like the 9, is a leader who is drawn to careers such as politics or science as avenues to bring forth revolutionary ideas. Similar to the 8 vibration, they also desire to attain power and need to learn how to balance the spiritual and material worlds.

The life path number and expression number are similar to the core iris structure because they have the greatest impact on a person.

Astrology and Numerology

Each of the 12 zodiacal signs has a corresponding number that shares similar qualities.

> Aries = 1 Brave, courageous and pioneering.
> Taurus = 4 Stable, practical, methodical
> Gemini = 3 Expressive, versatile, quick-witted.
> Cancer = 6 Nurturing, compassionate, domestic, sensitive.
> Leo = 5 Adventurous, adaptable, charismatic, persuasive, dramatic.
> Virgo = 22 Practical, visionary, service-oriented, helpful.
> Libra = 2 Harmonious, cooperative, relationship oriented.
> Scorpio = 7 Truth seeker, inventive, loner, creative.
> Sagittarius = 5 Talkative, quick-minded, fun loving, versatile.
> Capricorn = 8 Money oriented, materialistic, hard workers, ambitious.
> Aquarius = 9 Humanitarian, altruistic, future oriented.
> Pisces = 11 Cooperative, intuitive, compassionate.

The following planets reveal similar traits to these number calculations:

> Sun sign = Life path number
> Moon = Expression number
> Cooperative aspects = Day of birth
> Saturn, challenging aspects and the North Node = Karmic lessons
> Saturn Return = Challenge #2 (arriving mid-life)
> Second Saturn Return = Challenge #4 (age 58)
> Venus = Heart's desire number
> Mars = Hidden passion number

Palmistry and Astrology

The main correlation here is between the mounts, fingers and the planets. Each mount and finger is named after a planet and shares the same characteristics as that planet.

Mounts/fingers = planets
The 7 mounts identified on a hand correspond to the following planets: Sun, Mercury, Saturn, Jupiter, Venus, Mars, and the Moon. The fingers relate to the first four planets mentioned.

There is also a similarity between the four hand types, the elements, and the corresponding zodiacal signs.

> Fire hand = Fire element (Aries, Leo and Sagittarius)
> Earth hand = Earth element (Taurus, Virgo and Capricorn)
> Air hand = Air element (Gemini, Libra, Aquarius)
> Water hand = Water element (Cancer, Scorpio, Pisces)

The lines on the hand correspond to the four most prominent planets.

> Life line = Sun (main approach to life)
> Heart line = Moon (emotional nature)
> Head line = Mercury (way of thinking)
> Saturn line = Saturn (career ambitions)

Palmistry and Numerology

The similarity between these two influences is seen in the hand lines, which correspond to certain number calculations.

> Life = Life path number
> Heart = Expression number

Head = Life path and expression number
Saturn line = Heart's desire number

The following hand types reveal similar traits to these numbers:
Fire hand =   1,3,5
Earth hand = 4, 8, 22
Air hand =   2,7, 9
Water hand = 6,11

COMPARING RESULTS

Comparing the results of the various approaches to self-awareness helps us isolate karmic lessons and gifts and talents, the two major components in our life purpose. In comparing results, we should consider the following areas:

Similar Lessons

A lesson that appears in two places indicates that we must exert extra effort in mastering this lesson. Remember, the more challenging the lesson, the more opportunity for growth.

What are the similar lessons for someone with the Sun sign Pisces and a Flower iris constitution? The former offers the lesson of gaining emotional clarity and learning to discriminate one's thoughts from those of others. The latter's lesson is to focus the emotions to gain more stability in life and master self-expression. In both cases, there is a need to understand the emotional energies and overcome emotional confusion.

Mergers

Mergers occur when characteristics within one approach, or in two or more approaches to self-awareness, influence or compliment each other. These highlighted characteristics—perhaps talents or skills—should be considered when formulating a life purpose statement.

Let's take a look at someone with a harmony ring and a numerology life path number of 2. The influence of the Ring of Harmony is to seek harmony among family members and groups. The desire for harmony often leads to efforts to improve humanity, such as joining social welfare groups. Life path 2's influence is to bring peace and cooperation among people, to create a harmonious world. This situation illustrates the desire for harmony, which is enhanced by both influences. This individual may have exceptional people skills and diplomatic talents.

Diffusers

Diffusers are opposite influences within one approach or in two or more different approaches to self-awareness. Like mergers, diffusers reveal special gifts and talents. The key is to find the point of balance—where the gift resides—between the two opposing tendencies. We can achieve balance by incorporating a little of each quality, perhaps lessening the emphasis of one and adding more of another, until the two opposing influences meet halfway. Like a pendulum, people often swing between the two extremes. Awareness helps them see where they are out of balance and how to restore balance.

What about someone with a core iris constitution of Shaker and a Virgo Sun sign? Shaker points to a radical person, one who strives to go beyond the norms of society. This person has great vision and is capable of leading others to help fulfill his expansive visions. Virgo describes a practical, logical, methodical person, one who is industrious and serious, but perhaps narrow-minded.

The expansiveness of the Shaker decreases the narrow-minded tendencies of the Virgo, while Virgo's practical qualities bring the Shaker back down to earth. It creates a practical framework for manifesting Shaker's visions in the physical world. In this case, balance would result in being a practical visionary, using the gift of practicality to manifest grand visions.

Before you practice putting your own puzzle pieces together, read the following case study. I've used myself as the subject of this study.

CASE STUDY

PART I: GATHERING THE PIECES

Over a six-year period, I searched for my life purpose using the approaches explained in this book. Through this process I came to appreciate how various influences interact and how they affect me. I also began to notice similarities in the various pieces of information that I uncovered. For example, I received a Rayid iris analysis shortly after receiving my astrological natal chart. I was struck by how much both sets of information paralleled each other.

Would this correlation continue with other approaches as well? Not only did the correlation hold, but I found that these repeated (similar) lessons are of utmost significance. In addition, I learned that influences may be enhanced (mergers) as often as they are challenged or lessened (diffusers).

Note: I've omitted the approaches to self-awareness that did not support the lesson or talent described.

Past Life Influences
1. Gifts and talents: I learned: determination, concentration, goal setting, good verbal and written communication skills, healing, responsibility, and will-power.
2. Karmic lessons: I need to be objective, understand my emotional energies, be empathetic instead of sympathetic, and expand my vision to see the big picture and avoid fragmented thinking.

Astrology
1. Gifts and talents: I am creative, versatile, multitalented, and a quick learner. I have good written and verbal communication skills, strong reasoning ability, expansive thinking, and visionary ideas.
2. Karmic lessons: I must learn to be self-assertive, love and accept myself, and be independent. I tend to be overly self-critical and allow others to take advantage of me. I need to focus my energies and see the big picture.

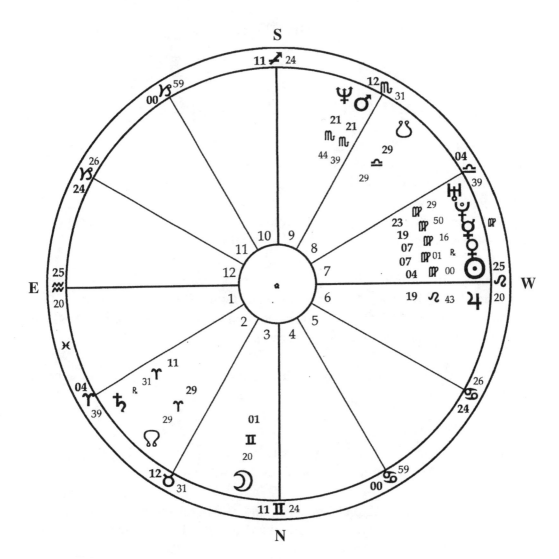

Numerology

1. Life path number: 22
2. Expression number: 6
3. Gifts and talents: I use practicality and vision to manifest unique ideas in the physical world. I am creative, cooperative, nurturing, and want to be of service. I have a good intellect and am intuitive. I have leadership potential.
4. Karmic lessons: My karmic numbers are 3, 4, and 6; challenge numbers: 1, 3, and 4.

	Creative	Vacillating	Balanced	Numbers of Letters
Physical				0
Mental	A A A	H N N N	G	8
Emotional	R	T		2
Intuitive	K	Y Y		3
	5	7	1	

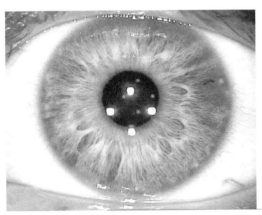 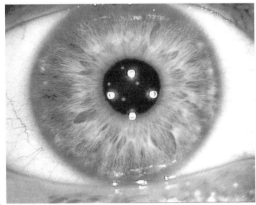

Left   *Right*

Rayid Iris

1. Iris constitution: Flower
2. Rings: Ring of Harmony
3. Hemispheric dominance: right brain
4. Introversion and extroversion: extrovert
5. Core positional traits: solitude, enlightenment, perfection, creativity, spiritual seeker.
6. Gifts and talents: I am influential, creative, joyous, visionary, sociable, versatile, service oriented, and harmonious.
7. Karmic lessons: I need to focus my energy, trust myself, set boundaries, and be less cynical.

Palmistry

1. Gifts and talents: I have a strong mind, good intellect. I am determined, ambitious, courageous, and a good communicator.
2. Karmic lessons: I need to blend my intellect and my feelings and be more decisive.

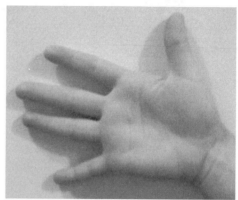

Family/Birth Order

1. Gifts and talents: My family helped me gain reasoning skills, common sense, an understanding of proper social behavior, a strong set of values, and how to get along in the physical world. I am the second born girl with the gifts of a sharp mind, creativity, imagination, and determination.
2. Karmic lessons: I need to be less critical, love myself, blend logic and feelings to fulfill my desires, develop willpower and a sense of peace within.

PART II: SIMILAR KARMIC LESSONS

Similar Karmic Lesson 1: I need to set boundaries for myself.

1. Astrology: The six mutable signs in my natal chart create the tendency to be too flexible, acquiescing to what other people want. The North Node in Aries tells me I need to be more independent and speak my mind. Jupiter makes a challenging aspect to Neptune, so I must prevent my strong desire to rescue people from turning me into a victim or martyr.
2. Numerology: Challenge number 1 represents my need to be independent and stand up for my beliefs. To overcome this challenge, I must trust myself, build my own value system, and adhere to it.
3. Rayid iris: The harmony ring shows that, in a desperate attempt to maintain peace and harmony, I may overwork myself, accept negative behavior to avoid conflict, and take on other people's problems.
4. Palmistry: The Girdle of Venus shows that I am overly eager to please, allowing myself to be taken advantage of.

Benefits: I have learned to say "no" before I overextend myself and to uphold my beliefs. I value my thoughts more, holding firm, as needed, when they are challenged. I also speak my mind more. I no longer burn the candle at both ends. I take more time to make decisions. I accept that sometimes saying "no" may lead to conflict.

Similar Karmic Lesson 2: I must be less critical of myself and of others.

1. Past life influences: A past life profile—I was a female in France in the 1300s—reflected my tendency to be critical of myself. I measured myself by how much I could produce and transferred this attitude to my children by criticizing them when they did not live up to my expectations.
2. Astrology: Sun, Venus, Mercury, and Pluto in Virgo (seventh house); North Node in Aries. I tend to be perfectionistic and critical of myself and of others. I need to love and accept myself and others, stop striving for perfection, and not base my self-worth on others' opinions.
3. Numerology: Karmic lesson 3; challenge number 3. I need to overcome self-criticism, refrain from setting standards I can never meet, and be easier on myself.
4. Rayid iris: Flower in position number 16: self-esteem and spirit. I am impatient with myself and have perfectionist tendencies. I have the potential for creative talents, yet they are blocked due to low self-esteem. I need to trust and accept myself.
5. Family: A family past life profile revealed that all my family members were highly judgmental. The suggestion was for each family member to be less critical of the others and practice unconditional acceptance.

Benefits: I have seen how destructive it is to criticize myself and others. To remedy this, I use positive affirmations. I validate myself for all my good qualities and accomplishments and do nice things for myself. I no longer attract people who are critical of me. Following the process in this book has boosted my self-esteem by helping me become aware of many of my talents so I can express my creativity to the fullest.

Similar Karmic Lesson 3: I need to focus.

1. Past life influences: A past life profile showed that I often started out on one path and eventually swayed from it. For example, in a past life in Spain, I was chosen from among my many brothers and sisters to attend school. I loved learning and planned to study for many years. However, I let a relationship pull me off course and I left school to get married. My dharma (an individual's spiritual duty) is, therefore, steadfastness. To fulfill my dharma I need to be focused and steadfast in my spiritual studies.

2. Astrology: Moon in Gemini; six mutable signs; Mars makes a challenging aspect to Jupiter. My curiosity and desire for adventure pull me in many different directions, scattering energies, and adding restlessness, which makes it difficult for me to make commitments. I carry flexibility and cooperation to an extreme instead of following my own ideals.
3. Numerology: Karmic lesson 4. I need to find a direction in life, stick with it, and build a foundation.
4. Rayid iris: Flower iris pattern. I am flexible and prefer change. I am excited at the beginning of projects, yet this enthusiasm often doesn't last to the end of the project. Energies tend to be scattered.
5. Palmistry: I have a short life line which reflects my desire for freedom and variety.

Benefits: I have learned to chose one area and expand within it. In college, I combined my interests in economics, political science, history, and foreign languages and created my own major: Comparative International Economics. I have also combined many facets of health and healing into my practice, including herbs, nutrition, mind/body therapies, massage, and emotional release work. I have combined my metaphysical and healing interests through writing, lecturing, and teaching on health and spirituality. To remain happy and enthusiastic, I need to commit to one thing that allows expansion and variety.

Similar Karmic Lesson 4: I need to help others—and myself—by empowering them with empathy rather than enable them with sympathy.

1. Past life influences: By being too sympathetic, I have been an enabler. My lesson is to be less sympathetic and more empathetic, thereby empowering rather than enabling people.
2. Astrology: North node in Aries; five planets in the seventh house; Jupiter makes a challenging aspect to Neptune. These influences signal the overwhelming desire to achieve harmony at any price, hence, the tendency to want to save other people.
3. Numerology: Expression number 6. I meddle too much in other people's business, trying to solve their problems, depriving them of the opportunity to work through their own challenges.
4. Rayid iris: Ring of harmony. I sympathize with and take on other people's problems, feeling that I need to solve them all.
5. Palmistry: Curve of Venus. To avoid pain and suffering I will rescue people from difficult situations.

Benefits: I have changed the way I serve others. I am more empowered as I teach people the tools to help themselves. In turn, they teach others, creating a domino effect. I no longer feel worn out from trying to solve everyone's problems.

PART III: MERGERS

Merger 1: I am creative.

1. Past life influences: I have developed good verbal and written skills.
2. Astrology: Moon in Gemini; Uranus makes a cooperative aspect to Neptune; Mercury makes a unifying aspect to Venus; Jupiter in Leo. I am drawn towards artistic and literary professions. I have a unique artistic or creative talent. I am original and imaginative. My gift to the world involves blending emotions, fantasy, and rationality with logic. I have the ability to add beauty to language, making me a gifted writer.
3. Numerology: Life path number 22; expression number 6. I have the ability to manifest creative ideas in the world. I have artistic and musical talents, with creativity in the visual fields. My date of birth (27) stresses creative talent.
4. Rayid iris: Flower iris pattern; flower in position number 15. I have abundant creative potential, perhaps manifesting itself in a career in acting, art, music, or writing.
5. Family/birth order: My very creative mother taught me the importance of developing my creativity. Both parents encouraged me to develop my creative writing skills. I possess the creative and imaginative mind of the number two girl.
6. Palmistry: My long Sun finger allows me to easily tap into my creativity.

Benefits: I have used this knowledge to boost my self-confidence and my belief in my creative abilities. I always imagined myself writing movies. When an astrologer told me my career could involve the media and entertainment industry I was encouraged and have since taken a film course and written my first screenplay. I have fashioned my career around creative pursuits. I also realized that I work best in an unstructured environment, so I have chosen career paths where I am independent and have the freedom to create.

Merger 2: I have a strong desire to aid and heal others.

1. Past life influences: During one lifetime in England I was a nurse who adopted a young orphan with tuberculosis. I nursed him back to health and raised him to be

a healthy adult. During another lifetime in England I was able to attend school, an opportunity not available to many females during the1700s. I was a veterinarian who used herbs, poultices, and body manipulations to heal animals. As a healer in Egypt in 800 B.C., I dedicated my life to learning spiritual and scientific methods of healing. I learned about forms, structure, and energy. I experimented with conducting different forms of energy through my body and projecting this energy to plants and people.

2. Astrology: Sun in Virgo; Jupiter in Leo (sixth house); Mars makes a cooperative aspect to Pluto. I want to be of service. I am interested in health, healing, and hygiene, and in serving as some type of healer. I am willing to fight courageously against negativity to make the world a better place.
3. Numerology: Expression number 6. I am very loving and compassionate and want to bring harmony into the world. I am good at healing and at resolving conflicts.
4. Rayid iris: Harmony ring. I want to heal—and bring peace and harmony to—family, friends, and the world. To accomplish this, I may join environmental groups and fight for justice. I may become involved in the healing arts, counseling, and social work. However, I must first heal myself to gain the strength to heal the world.
5. Palmistry: Curve of Venus. I help people to avoid pain and suffering.

Benefits: I serve through teaching and healing, which reconfirms that I am on the right path. I have learned that by teaching the Universal Truths I can be of the greatest service to others. I can aid large groups of people indirectly through my writing and lecturing. I have also learned that the best way I can help people is to empathize with and empower them.

Merger 3: I seek spiritual wisdom.
1. Past life influences:
2. Astrology: Aquarius rising; Neptune in Scorpio (ninth house); Mars makes a cooperative aspect to Pluto; Uranus makes a cooperative aspect to Neptune; Neptune makes a cooperative aspect with Pluto. I am drawn to spirituality, research, and investigative fields. I am open and sensitive to dreams, spirituality, and intuition. I look for new ways of doing things in religion, politics, and writing. I want to inspire the world and work to better the human condition.
3. Numerology: Life path number 22. I am a master builder, combining practicality and vision.
4. Rayid iris: Flowers in both eyes in positions 23 and 24 indicate that I enjoy solitude and have a strong interest in spiritual study. I also have psychic abilities.

5. Family/birth order: My birth position of second born girl indicates I enjoy retreating into the mystical and spiritual realms.

Benefits: I realized that my soul has a strong urge to learn the true meaning of "self." I continue my spiritual studies. I have learned to use my interest in spirituality to apply my life purpose and be of service to others (teaching metaphysics) and be creative (writing books and movies about spiritual principles).

Merger 4: I work well with others in partnerships.
1. Astrology: Five planets in the seventh house; south node in Libra; Neptune makes a cooperative aspect to Pluto; Jupiter on the descent. There will be much emphasis on working with others in various types of partnerships. The Libra influence shows the capacity to cooperate and harmonize with others.
2. Numerology: Expression number 6. I am a loving, caring, and nurturing person. I work well in "people" professions such as teaching, counseling, and healing.
3. Rayid iris: Flower iris constitution; ring of harmony. I am a social person who brings joy and vision to social situations. I strive to attain a sense of peace and harmony among people.
4. Family/birth order: I learned to share and cooperate, and to harmonize with different personalities.
5. Palmistry: A long heart line and a wide life line. I am an extrovert who can connect with people on an emotional level.

Benefits: I have incorporated my desire to help and be with people into my career. I work with people to improve their health and well-being and empower them so that they can live the most rewarding life possible.

Merger 5: I have good written and verbal communication skills.
1. Past life influences: I have developed good communication skills.
2. Astrology: Moon in Gemini in the third house; five planets in Virgo. My chart shows that there will be much emphasis on communication from the third house, as well as a strong Mercury presence (Mercury rules Virgo).
3. Rayid iris: Flower iris constitution. I have the gift of communicating with emotion and enthusiasm.
4. Palmistry: Prominent mount of Mercury. I have good communication skills.

Benefits: Realizing that I chose these influences of communication has encouraged me and validated my dream of a career in writing and public speaking.

PART IV: DIFFUSERS

Diffuser 1: My mind and emotions often conflict. Balance point: I can combine logic and feelings to make wise decisions.

1. Astrology: Neptune in the ninth house; heavy influence of Mercury; Aquarius rising; two planets in Scorpio; Moon in Gemini; Sun makes a challenging aspect to the Moon; Moon makes a challenging aspect to Mercury; Jupiter makes a challenging aspect to Neptune. My challenge is to rationalize less and blend the heart and the head. I seek transcendence through religion, philosophy, and higher education, but need to stay levelheaded to avoid getting emotionally carried away to the point of escape or self-delusion. I can achieve my goals by using both passion and logic.
2. Numerology: I am strongest in the mental plane and weaker in the physical and emotional planes. I approach life from a predominantly mental perspective. To create balance I need to still my mind and connect with my intuition.
3. Rayid iris: Flower iris structure. I experience life predominantly through the emotions. I need to add logic and reasoning to my decision making and to other thought processes.
4. Palmistry: My right hand shows my determination to work hard, be productive, and achieve many goals. My left hand reveals my desire to spend more time cultivating personal relationships. My challenge is to blend my work and personal life.

Benefits: I have learned to cultivate my intuition so that I feel confident relying on its messages, combining them with my reasoning skills. I meditate daily and practice other spiritual disciplines that help me to still my mind so that I can listen to my feelings and understand my emotions. When I have difficulty making a decision I write out my thoughts on paper or discuss them with a friend. Verbalizing my thoughts helps me see more clearly. If I rely too much on logic, I do some physical activity or get a massage. This helps me feel grounded and connects me with my emotions. When my mind and emotions conflict I often gain perspective by looking at the whole picture objectively, rather than fixating on one small point.

Diffuser 2: My opposing tendencies are to be practical and to be visionary. Balance point: I am a practical visionary capable of manifesting concepts into reality.

1. Past life influences: In England in the 1700s, I was a visionary woman who went beyond what was acceptable for women by learning to read and write. I pursued my interest in animals by searching for people who could teach me about veterinary medicine. I had a vision of becoming a doctor and I attained this goal,

something quite out of the ordinary for women at the time. I also had the more traditional and practical desires to marry and have a family. After practicing veterinary medicine, I married and had five children. I left my practice to raise my children, causing some inner conflict because I enjoyed my work so much. The karma from that lifetime was to learn how to blend my visionary and practical desires without feeling that I had to sacrifice one thing for another. During another lifetime in Egypt in 800 B.c., I fled an arranged marriage to study esoteric healing in a cloistered environment. I dedicated my life to spiritual and scientific study, and learned to be a conductor of energy.

2. Astrology: Sun in Virgo; Aquarius on the Ascendant; Neptune in the ninth house; Venus in Virgo in the seventh house; Uranus in the seventh house; Jupiter makes a challenging aspect to Neptune. I am a visionary with high ideals for humanity. I transcend the mundane physical world through the study of spirituality, religion, and philosophy. I express myself rationally and practically and I want common sense in my relationships. It is through relationships that my urge for freedom and unconventionality will shine. I am progressive and inventive. I have very high ideals; when my visions do not match reality I feel frustrated.

3. Numerology: Life path number 22; challenge number 4. Sometimes I live in a fantasy world and conceive ideas that are not sound. Other times, I am practical to the point of narrow-mindedness. My challenge is to integrate practicality and vision. If I am overly practical I will shut out my visions; if I am too logical, my ideas will lack a visionary quality.

4. Rayid iris: Ring of harmony; right brain dominance. I am a visionary with high ideals for a better world. I have high expectations and ideals for myself and for humanity. My gift is the power of influence: I can use this to change the world.

5. Family/birth order: Both my parents were very practical, down-to-earth people. They taught me how to reason and to apply common sense to my endeavors. I possess the vivid imagination and keen mind of the number two girl.

6. Palmistry: Earth hand; curved head line. I have a practical temperament combined with an imaginative mind.

Benefits: I have often felt pulled in two directions in my career and in relationships, trying to balance my practical and visionary sides. I have wanted to earn a lot of money in a job that is practical, stable, and financially lucrative. On the other hand, I want to do what I love, which is riskier. One part of me desires an unconventional life in service to humanity; another part desires marriage and family.

Diffuser 3: My opposing tendencies are to focus too narrowly on details and to be overly expansive with impractical ideas. Balance point: I can see how various pieces fit together and make a whole.

1. Astrology: Four planets and Sun in Virgo. The heavy Virgo influence offers the ability to focus on and work with details, seeing the pieces needed to make up a whole. Aquarius rising: I have expansive visions and great dreams for humanity. Jupiter in Leo: I have breadth of vision and expansive thinking. I desire to contribute to life on a grand scale, but can become reckless without regard to detail.
2. Numerology: Life path 22; karmic lesson 4. I am capable of forming expansive visions. I also need to be more organized, recognize the importance of details, and steps necessary to build a foundation.
3. Rayid iris: Right brain dominance. I have a difficulty with details, which leads to disorganization.

Benefits: I enjoy learning new concepts and theories, from health and nutrition to metaphysics. I look at the details of what I learn and from them glean the universal concept to benefit humanity. This book is an example of how I studied various approaches to self-awareness and saw the universal thread that ties them together.

PART V: SUGGESTIONS FOR GROWTH

1. Learn to set boundaries for myself: Any type of martial arts, particularly tai chi, would be beneficial. These exercises build strength and security and help people get in touch with their personal power so that they can control and direct their energy.
2. Overcome self-criticism: List my positive qualities. Ask others to tell me what qualities they like in me. Convert these to affirmations and say them daily. Engage in activities that allow me to express my talents in some way to boost self-confidence. Avoid toxic, critical people.
3. Develop and use my creative energy: Engage in some form of creative activity each day.
4. Emphasize learning through relationships: Continue doing self-development work to gain a positive self-image and maintain my individuality in relationships.
5. Balance intellect and feelings: Engage in physical exercise daily, especially tai chi, yoga, and bioenergetic exercises. These help me ground the body, move out of intellectualism and in touch with my intuition. Reflexology and massage are also good for balancing the mind and emotions.
6. Learn to focus: Still the mind with activities such as meditation, chanting, and concentration exercises.

ASSEMBLE YOUR OWN PUZZLE

PART I: GATHERING THE PIECES

Use the information you have gathered to create your own case study.

Past Life Influences

Information from Akashic records or past life regression session:

Gifts and talents built in past lives:

Karmic lessons:

Astrology
Insert your astrology chart
Gifts and talents:

Karmic lessons:

Numerology
Insert your Planes of Expression chart
Life path number:

Expression number:

Gifts and talents:

Karmic lessons:

Rayid Iris

Insert iris photos

Iris constitution:

Rings:

Hemispheric dominance:

Introversion, extroversion:

Gifts and talents:

Karmic lessons:

Palmistry
Insert palm photos
Gifts and talents:

Karmic lessons:

Family/Birth Order

Gifts and talents:

Karmic lessons:

PART II: SIMILAR KARMIC LESSONS

Remember that the number of similar lessons, mergers, and diffusers varies with the individual. You may need to photocopy the forms provided to accommodate additional information.

Similar Lesson 1:

Past life influences:

Astrology:

Numerology:

Rayid iris:

Palmistry:

Family/Birth order:

Benefits:

Similar Lesson 2:

Past life influences:

Astrology:

Numerology:

Rayid iris:

Palmistry:

Family/Birth order:

Benefits:

Similar Lesson 3:

Past life influences:

Astrology:

Numerology:

Rayid iris:

Palmistry:

Family/Birth order:

Benefits:

PART III: MERGERS

Merger 1:

Past life influences:

Astrology:

Numerology:

Rayid iris:

Palmistry:

Family/Birth order:

Benefits:

Merger 2:

Past life influences:

Astrology:

Numerology:

Rayid iris:

Palmistry:

Family/Birth order:

Benefits:

Merger 3:

Past life influences:

Astrology:

Numerology:

Rayid iris:

Palmistry:

Family/Birth order:

Benefits:

PART IV: DIFFUSERS

Diffuser 1:

Past life influences:

Astrology:

Numerology:

Rayid iris:

Palmistry:

Family/Birth order:

Benefits:

Diffuser 2:

Past life influences:

Astrology:

Numerology:

Rayid iris:

Palmistry:

Family/Birth order:

Benefits:

Diffuser 3:

Past life influences:

Astrology:

Numerology:

Rayid iris:

Palmistry:

Family/Birth order:

Benefits:

PART V: SUGGESTIONS FOR GROWTH

Suggestion 1:

Suggestion 2:

Suggestion 3:

Suggestion 4:

Suggestion 5:

Suggestion 6:

Nine

Part One
Identifying the Purpose:
Gifts and Talents

In Chapter 8, we assembled the puzzle pieces and grouped them in three categories: similar lessons, mergers, and diffusers. We have discovered our gifts and talents. Now we will learn how to fulfill the first part of our life purpose: finding ways to give of ourselves using our gifts and talents. To do this, we must create a life purpose statement. This statement will take into account our gifts and talents and will help us find the career that will serve as a vehicle through which we can fulfill our life purpose.

THE LIFE PURPOSE STATEMENT

A life purpose statement incorporates the strengths revealed in mergers and diffusers. It must have a central focus, yet be broad and flexible, adapting to a person's desire for expansion and variety, with the freedom to choose from among many different activities.

We may need to be creative in discovering ways to expand within the parameters of our life purpose statement. The concepts in Chapter 11 will help us expand our creativity.

Review the results of my case study. Then, list the mergers and diffusers in sections III and IV of your case study. Based on this information, write a life purpose statement.

MY CASE STUDY RESULTS

Mergers

1. I am creative.
2. I have a strong desire to aid and heal others.
3. I seek spiritual wisdom.
4. I work well with others in partnerships.
5. I have good written and verbal communication skills.

Diffusers

1. My mind and emotions often conflict. Balance point: I can combine logic and feelings to make wise decisions.
2. My opposing tendencies are to be practical and to be visionary. Balance point: I am a practical visionary capable of manifesting concepts into reality.
3. My opposing tendencies are to focus too narrowly on details and to be overly expansive with impractical ideas. Balance point: I can see how various pieces fit together and make a whole.

Life Purpose Statement

My life purpose is to influence and empower humanity by teaching metaphysical truths and visionary health concepts in creative ways through written and verbal communication.

Note that my statement does not mention a specific career. It is simply a broad structure under which I can expand to do many different things. I have the freedom to bring cutting-edge health and metaphysical knowledge to the world in diverse ways, such as by writing books and screenplays, lecturing, and teaching. Since I like variety, I use my imagination to find more diverse ways of serving the world. (It helps that my areas of interest—health and metaphysics—are unlimited in scope. I have found, though, that any field is unlimited when you use your imagination.)

CAREER

Since few of us are financially independent, our careers may be the main avenue through which we can fulfill our life purpose. What's more, we all want satisfying jobs—those geared to fulfilling our life purpose. So, we will work on creating a life purpose statement that incorporates jobs as a vehicle to achieve that purpose.

People often find it difficult to mold their life purpose statement to reflect a traditional career or job. Because of their narrow focus and rigid guidelines, traditional jobs can present a challenge for creative people. We may need to be creative and formulate our own jobs.

What happens when our life purpose cannot be fulfilled through a high-paying, stable job? Don't worry. *Remember, when you do what you love, the money will follow. Success comes from taking risks.*

I translated my life purpose statement (to influence and empower humanity by teaching metaphysical truths and visionary health concepts in creative ways through written and verbal communication.) into a vocation by writing books on metaphysics and health; writing screenplays; and speaking in public on self-awareness and health issues. In fact, this book is a manifestation of my life purpose. I used my talent of seeing how all the methods of self-awareness fit together into the big picture. I then communicated this in writing to teach people how to become more self-aware and find their life purpose.

A New Direction

Forty-four-year-old Reid was looking for a new direction in life. He was a multitalented engineer, with experiences from home remodeling to managing companies. Reid sought guidance in career choices; he wanted to share his professional talents.

When Reid learned that his highest potential was to blaze a new trail, he found new energy and encouragement in his career. His shaker-flower iris structure reflects the characteristics of an original thinker who is not afraid to pierce the boundaries of tradition. His expression number 1 makes him a natural leader, explorer, and innovator.

The life purpose statement for Reid embodies this potential: "Lead and inspire groups of people to help bring innovative concepts and inventions into the world that will improve humanity and the planet in areas such as technology and ecology." "Yes," he responded. "This fits me well."

A week later, Reid was excited about the insight he had about his life purpose. He wanted to bring alternative forms of energy to the world and to help clean up the environment. With new resolution, Reid is pursuing a new career.

The Career Profile chart below is designed to guide you in determining which career best matches your life purpose.

1. For each approach, put a check next to the profession (or professions) that would use the gifts and talents specified in Part I: Gathering the Pieces of your case study. For example, the professions of writer and doctor would help me use my gifts, named under "Past Life Influences," of good verbal and written communication skills and healing. The gifts and talents listed under "Astrology" (creative, good written and verbal communication skills, strong reasoning ability, and visionary ideas) point to teacher, writer, and actor. Note: Use the blanks provided for professions not listed.
2. After you complete each column, add the number of checks in each row. Write the total number in the last column.
3. The professions with the greatest number of checks are those most closely aligned with your life purpose.

CAREER PROFILE CHART

	Past Life	Astrology	Numerology	Rayid Iris	Palmistry	TOTAL
Accountant						
Actor						
Detective						
Doctor						
Engineer						
Psychologist						
Scientist						
Teacher						
Veterinarian						
Writer						

TASKS

1. List your mergers.

2. List your diffusers.

3. Create a life purpose statement based on the above information.

QUESTIONS

1. Which strengths and talents would you like to acquire?
2. Describe your ideal career. How closely does it match your life purpose statement?
3. What sign is on your Midheaven?
4. In what house is the planetary ruler of the Midheaven sign? Based on this, in what area will your vocation reside?
5. What careers are associated with the house where the planetary ruler of the Midheaven sign resides?

EXERCISES

1. Based on your life purpose statement generate a list of suitable careers.
2. Help someone else formulate a life purpose statement and a list of suitable careers.
3. Reflect on your childhood through age seven. Write about this experience.
4. Make a list of desires. Trace the origin of each to an influence explained in one of the six approaches.

Ten

Part Two
Identifying the Purpose:
Learning Lessons

Creating a life purpose statement has brought us halfway to fulfilling that purpose. In addition to sharing our gifts and talents, we must also work through our karmic lessons, identified in Chapter 10. This chapter, Part II of "Identifying the Purpose," offers ways to move through lessons with ease and gain the most understanding from them.

Each time we learn a lesson, we add wisdom to the soul, relieving some karma and moving one step closer to wholeness. Wisdom includes characteristics such as loyalty, honesty, cooperation, compassion, service, and integrity. Each incarnation brings an increasingly larger reservoir of wisdom we can call on.

When we resist or ignore a lesson, we resist the urges of our soul and slow the soul's progress toward fulfilling its purpose. The more we allow the soul to guide us, the more easily we can embrace lessons. Lessons we avoid will not go away; they simply reappear in a more dominant manner. Recurring unlearned lessons drain our energy and detract from our ability to serve the world.

When we are aware of our lessons, we are not caught off guard. Awareness prepares us to better deal with lessons as they appear. When faced with a difficult situation, we can empower ourselves to accept the lesson with gratitude, rather than retreat into self-pity, and to learn in the moment, rather than from hindsight. We can learn in one lifetime what previously may have taken several lifetimes. What's more, the knowledge we have gained allows us to set up conditions to learn the skills we lack. For example, if we need to learn leadership abilities, we can choose jobs that require management skills. We should congratulate ourselves on such remarkable progress!

Before you write your karmic lessons (revealed in Part II: Similar Karmic Lessons of the case study), study the following example, my karmic lessons derived from my case study:

1. I need to set boundaries for myself.
2. I must be less critical of myself and of others.
3. I need to focus.
4. I need to help others—and myself—by empowering them with empathy rather than enable them with sympathy.

LEARNING AWARENESS JOURNAL

When a troublesome situation occurs, we can study our karmic lessons to recognize the lessons inherent in that situation. This understanding allows us to work through the lessons quickly. The Learning Awareness Journal at the end of this chapter is a tool to help identify lessons and derive the greatest degree of learning from them.

At age 28, I learned a profound lesson. Working through the learning awareness process taught me why the situation occurred and what my lesson was. My wish is that you use this process to learn from difficult situations and avoid recurring painful lessons.

As I continued to apply this process to other situations in my life, I realized that there is a fine line between lessons to be learned and detriments to our lives. I often lingered in unhealthy situations, believing that if I left I would be running from a lesson. Others may believe in staying in degrading situations to learn a lesson. What I discovered, however, is that the lesson itself is to gather the courage to leave.

Lessons avoided will recur, so it is important to determine when we still need to learn something and when it is time to move on. This process provides a structure to help us do just that. Read the following example to see how it works.

> *In financial difficulty, Juan, my longtime boyfriend, asked to borrow money from me for an investment. He assured me that he would repay the money by the end of the month. Although a bit skeptical, I loved him and wanted to help, so I lent him several thousand dollars. The investment deal was not success-*

> *ful. Rick did not keep his promise to repay me. Ex-*
> *tremely upset, I ended the relationship.*

I was hurt and sad. I trusted Juan and he let me down. I felt betrayed because he did not repay me. I was angry because I let this happen: even though I had concerns about the investment, I went along with it anyway. I was also angry because I had planned to use the money Juan borrowed to open my own business. As a result, I had to work another year to save more money. I acted on the belief that one must always help others in need.

Past Life: In a past life with Juan, I was his mother. I was a nurse who adopted him to help him regain his health (he had tuberculosis). I was successful and raised him to be a healthy adult. The past life crossing report stated that in the present lifetime I once again was attempting to save Juan from what I considered unpleasant experiences. I was actually depriving him of important lessons that he needed to experience. Lending him the money did not help him learn responsibility and financial management. By trying to save him from going into debt I worsened his situation and caused problems for myself as well. The lesson in the report was for me to respect Juan by letting him work through his own problems rather than bailing him out.

Astrology: The seven mutable signs in my chart mean I am flexible to the point of trying to please others without considering how my actions will affect me. My South Node is in Libra: I want to harmonize with and please others, sometimes sympathizing with and enabling them rather than teaching them to be independent. Neptune in the ninth house means my excessive faith can lead to gullibility and unnecessary sacrifices.

Numerology: My expression number 6 makes me a very loving and caring person. I want to harmonize with other people and aid them in their troubles. However, I tend to put my own needs behind those of others too often. In this case, I postponed my plans to open my own business, working another year to replace the money I lent to Juan. People with this expression number are inclined to meddle too much in others' affairs. I would have been better off letting Juan work out his own financial problems.

Rayid Iris: With a harmony ring, I seek harmony in life, especially in relationships. I lent Juan money to create more harmony for him and for our relationship. I did not think carefully about my decision to lend him the money; rather, my strong love for Juan caused me to throw logic out the window.

Palmistry: My love line has many markings, indicating that I will face many challenges in personal relationships. I also have the Curve of Venus which causes me to be sympathetic.

Next, I must determine which karmic lessons are being activated, as well as which diffusers need to be brought into balance. Refer to Chapter 10, Part II: Similar Karmic Lessons, and Part IV: Diffusers, to see which lessons and diffusers are applicable.

The karmic lessons that are applicable in this situation are twofold: I need to set boundaries for myself, and I need to help others—and myself—by empowering them with empathy rather than enable them with sympathy.

There is one applicable diffuser: Mind and emotions often conflict.

In the situation I described, it is clear that I was out of balance, making a decision based solely on emotions. This helped me see the need to balance my intellect and my feelings. Now, before I make a decision, I divide a paper into two columns, one labeled "Logical" and other labeled "Emotional." In the "Logical" column I put the logical reasons I should give Juan money. In the "Emotional" column, I write the emotional reasons I should give Juan money. A substantial difference in the numbers of reasons in both columns signals an imbalance of head and heart.

TASKS

1. Complete the Learning Awareness Journal to record what you learned from major events in your life.
2. Describe the opportunities you now have to add wisdom to your soul. For example, if you were recently promoted to a managerial position, you have the opportunity to build understandings in leadership.
3. Describe the karmic lessons that you can learn from the six approaches (past lives, astrology, numerology, Rayid, palmistry, family/birth order).

LEARNING AWARENESS JOURNAL

My experience or event was:

My thoughts and feelings were:

Core beliefs related to my thoughts are:

Awareness Components

Past life karma:

Astrology:

Numerology:

Rayid iris:

Palmistry:

Family background:

Describe the karmic lessons learned and the diffusers brought into balance:

QUESTIONS

1. Which experiences do you wish never happened?
2. How do you feel about these experiences after completing the Learning Awareness Journal?

EXERCISES

1. List situations and/or people that bring up karmic lessons for you. Describe how you will learn from these experiences.
2. Select three recent experiences. Apply the learning awareness process.
3. Examine an area in your life, such as work or relationships, with which you are not happy and that you want to change. Follow the learning awareness process to determine whether there is a lesson to be learned or if it is something that no longer serves you.

Eleven

Action: Living Our Life Purpose

Using the six approaches in this book, we have identified our life purpose and established which careers will help us reach that goal. We are now ready to live our life purpose—to manifest our desires. When we are aligned with our life purpose, we can look forward to a sense of peace and happiness.

MANIFESTING OUR DESIRES

Following is a step-by-step process to make your dreams reality.

1. Identify and write down what you want. Be specific. For example, if your life purpose is to teach creativity, name the profession you would like (e.g., art and music teacher). Include job conditions such as hours, pay, distance from work, and benefits.
2. Set goals to give the mind direction and break them down into the smallest steps possible. If you want to become a nutritionist, write down the steps you need to get there (e.g., research health schools, talk to people working in the natural health field, visit a nutritionist and begin improving your own health).
3. Visualize your desire daily, using all five senses. The more clearly you visualize, the sooner and the more precisely your desire will manifest itself.
4. Focus on the end result, not the process. Whatever you think about and give energy to will grow, so focus only on what you want. Doubts and fears will kill your desires. Thinking about *how* your desire will manifest itself can be very limiting. You may end up raising so much doubt that you become discouraged and abandon your desires.

Working through the various approaches may have changed how we think about ourselves, our lives, and the world. Aligning with our life purpose may require additional changes. Just as our thoughts are key to manifesting our desires, so do they help us change old behaviors and incorporate new ones to create the life we desire. Our thoughts must always be in alignment with what we want.

To change ourselves we must change our thoughts. This may seem straightforward and easy, however, we need to remember that many if not most of our thoughts have been ingrained in us for years. To overcome this challenge, we can begin by changing our actions. Let's consider the following process for change.

A PROCESS FOR CHANGE

1. Identify what needs to be changed. *I'm shy and afraid of people. I want to be outgoing and unafraid.*
2. Visualize how you want to change. Use all five senses to imagine the new you. *I see myself smiling at a group of strangers. I hear myself laughing, feeling as though I belong in the group.*
3. Change your actions. It is through experience that we change, so do something different. *I smile and force myself to say hello to someone sitting alone at a table in a restaurant.*
4. Change your words. If you want to be an outgoing person, describe yourself that way. The more you describe yourself as outgoing, rather than shy, the sooner you will believe it and exhibit outgoing behavior. *I am friendly and outgoing and reach out to make other people feel comfortable.*
5. Change your thoughts. In many cases this will occur naturally as you practice steps 3 and 4. *I think less about my fears than about ways to welcome others.*

Doing something different demonstrates to the mind that it can think differently. For example, the assumption that parachuting ends in death will change when we survive our first jump. We have broken a belief and replaced our original assumption. The more often we do something new or different, the closer we come to successfully retraining our minds.

A Change in the Air

Dana's low self-esteem led her to believe she was unattractive. As a result, Dana spent little time on her physical appearance. She was, in fact, a beautiful woman and a talented pianist. Lacking confidence in her abilities, she was too shy to play for an audience. Dana consulted a psychotherapist. The therapist suggested she do some things differently, such as wearing dresses more often, pampering herself more, and later, taking a part-time job playing piano.

She started taking baths, a luxury she never before afforded herself. She began to dress up more often, even while at home. Eventually, Dana spent her evenings playing piano at a restaurant. Diners complimented her and restaurant management was pleased with the crowds she drew. Slowly, she began to change the way she saw herself, which included feeling more feminine. Her confidence grew. By taking action, Dana initiated the change in her thoughts and increased her self-esteem.

We can change our actions in many ways: taking a trip, moving to another city, surrounding ourselves with new groups of people, taking a class, or taking up a new hobby. Traveling to a foreign country is an especially effective way to open up new ways of thinking. I spent two years living in Europe, one year in France and another in Spain. Exposure to these new cultures, new ways of looking at things, and new people helped me change my thinking about the way life was supposed to be lived. My views on family, for example, changed drastically as I saw close-knit families whose 18 year olds were not champing at the bit to leave home.

Drama and theater work offers a wonderful opportunity to change our thoughts. Taking on the persona of a character lets us open ourselves to new ways of thinking. Improvisation allows people to shed shyness and act without concern for what others may think. An actor who played the part of Jesus in a movie became much more religious. Another actor unlocked her romantic, vulnerable, feminine side after playing Shakespeare's Juliet.

Solitude can cause a significant shift in perception. As part of their training, shamans go through a life-altering event called a "vision quest." They spend several days alone outdoors in a secluded area, with minimal supplies. They encounter different parts of themselves and are challenged to surpass what they thought possible in order to survive.

Throughout our childhood we form values and beliefs about the world, which serve as the basis for most of the choices we make. By making choices based on a different belief and value systems is yet another way to initiate change.

Making a Real Choice

By the age of 40, Kenneth had been divorced twice. He was unemployed and in debt. Previously, Kenneth made choices in favor of his relationships at the expense of other areas of his life. As each relationship ended, he found himself worse off than before. He was unhappy with his life and knew something had to change.

Kenneth decided to make choices that would benefit his career. He worked in real estate and knew the importance of location. So, he moved to a new city with the best-selling markets and earning potential. Kenneth began taking real estate and financial planning classes and seminars. Within a year, he was the top-selling agent in his office and became financially stable for the first time in his life. Kenneth began to value his independence and functioned well, even without a woman in his life.

Another way to choose differently is to put memory and imagination to work. When faced with a choice, we can look at the past (memory) to see what worked—and what did not. We can then visualize (imagine) the ideal outcome as well as the consequences of our choices. For example, consider whether you should move from one part of the country to another. Picture yourself in your new setting during the next year, and for the next three, five, and ten years. If you like what you see, you can confidently make that choice. If not, you know it is not the right choice.

TIPS FOR CHANGE

Incorporate these tips to facilitate the changes you want to make.

1. Focus only on what you want (as opposed to what you do not want). Whatever you think about and give energy to will grow. Think positively: "I will balance effortlessly on the tightrope," not "I will not fall."
2. Find a replacement for old limiting behaviors and beliefs. For example, replace food binges with a new hobby or a weekly massage.

3. Consider the negative consequences of not changing. Realizing that staying the same will be detrimental may give you enough courage to change.

Once we make a change, we must reinforce new behaviors. We must continue to visualize ourselves practicing new behaviors and applaud ourselves for doing so. We must make it difficult to fall back to old ways. For example, to change a nurturing behavior from eating favorite foods to receiving massages, we can set up massage appointments for the next few months to avoid the temptation to skip them.

The journey is always about change and growth. You now have the tools to understand all facets of yourself. This knowledge is power. You can use this power to choose the road that will lead you to the fulfillment of your life purpose. May you enjoy the journey and the freedom to pursue your greatest desires.

TASKS

1. Act on fulfilling your life purpose by following the four steps of "Manifesting Your Desires" outlined in this chapter.
2. Engage in a new experience that you believe will cause an inner transformation. Examples include a trip, a vision quest, or a new hobby.
3. Try acting. Check out your local theater group or an improvisational acting company.

QUESTIONS

1. What do you want to change in your life?
2. How have you caused change in your life? What strategies have worked in the past?
3. Which changes have you found difficult to make? Which changes have you avoided?
4. How do you feel about the majority of changes you have made?
5. What values drive most of your major decisions, e.g., family, money, work?

EXERCISES

1. Tell as many people as possible about your life purpose and how you plan to implement it.
2. Make a list of changes you need to make to incorporate your life purpose.
3. Identify any thoughts that could prevent you from fulfilling your life purpose. Use the Process for Change to replace them with more positive thoughts.
4. List several significant choices you have made in the last year and the impact they have had on your life. Which values and beliefs did you base your choices on? Note any choices that you were unhappy with and describe what you would do differently in the future in similar situations.
5. Make a list of your belief systems. Decide which ones serve you and which ones no longer benefit you. Then make a list of new beliefs to replace the old ones. Repeat them to yourself daily.
6. Think of a major decision you may need to make. List two possible choices. Draw a time line illustrating the effects your first choice will have on your life in 1, 3, 5, and 10 years. Repeat this process for your second choice.
7. Formulate a plan to change three things in your life. Start with the new actions you will take.

8. Reflect on any activities, people, trips, or classes that caused a change within you. Identify what caused the transformation.

Twelve

Evolution: Planning the Next Life

Experience is our greatest asset in the process of evolution. At every moment, our thoughts and actions shape opportunities and circumstances to come.

Experiment. Broaden your experience by learning from others as well as from yourself. Spend time with those who have developed the qualities of the influences you want to understand. Experience a past life regression, talk with someone who has had a near death experience.

Do not become bound by your influences. Use free will to mold your influences to your needs and desires. Ask yourself, "Who do I want to be today?" Have fun creating yourself—become your own hero.

Many Life Purpose students ask me what happens when they find their life purpose. Some fear that once they complete their life mission, they will die. The contrary is true: following your life purpose usually increases your life span. The soul may withdraw from the body and start another life when we are *not* fulfilling our life mission.

Students also wonder whether completing their life mission means they are exempt from reincarnating in the physical world. It is difficult to determine when we have completed our journey on Earth. By focusing our energy on soul growth, we ensure continual evolution. When we die, we will have the opportunity to review how we spent our life and decide if we need another lifetime to complete our learning.

Imagine constructing a tower of building blocks, each block representing a new talent or understanding you have mastered. How many blocks can you add in this lifetime? Practice these skills and talents, apply them, teach them to others. They will become a permanent part of your soul, the foundation for your next life.

When your tower reaches the sky, you will be ready to move to other planes of existence.

I wish you joy and happiness on your journey in this world and beyond.

CARPE DIEM

Recommended Resourses

If you wish to explore in greater depth any of the areas we've touched on, consider consulting the following books, Web sites, and other resources.

BOOKS

PAST LIVES

Todeschi, Kevin. *Edgar Cayce on the Akashic Records* (Virginia Beach, VA: A.R.E. press, 1998).

Wambach, Helen. *Reliving Past Lives: The Evidence Under Hypnosis* (New York, NY: Harper & Row, 1978).

Weiss, Brian L. *Many Lives, Many Masters* (New York, NY: Simon & Schuster, 1988).

Condron, Barbara, ed. *Uncommon Knowledge: An Introduction To Past Life & Health Readings.* (Windyville, MO: SOM Publishing, 1996).

Condron, Barbara, ed. *Work of the Soul: Past Life Recall & Spiritual Enlightenment.* (Windyville, MO: SOM Publishing, 1996).

Shroder, Tom. *Old Souls: The Scientific Evidence for Past Lives* (New York, NY: Simon & Schuster, 1999).

ASTROLOGY

Schermer, Barbara. *Astrology Alive: A Guide to Experiential Astrology and the Healing Arts* (Freemont, CA: The Crossing Press, 1998)

Lamb, Terry. *Born to Be Together: Love, Relationships and the Soul* (Carlsbad, CA: Hay House , Inc., 1998).

Marks, Tracy. *Your Secret Self: Illuminating the Mysteries of the Twelfth House* (Sebastopol, CA: CRCS Publications, 1989).

Pottenger, Maritha. *Easy Astrology Guide: How to Read Your Horoscope* (San Diego, CA: ACS Publications, 1996).

Spiller, Jan. *Astrology For The Soul* (New York, NY: Bantam Books, 1997).

NUMEROLOGY

Campbell, Florence. Your Days Are Numbered (Marina Del Rey, CA: DeVorss & Company, 1931, 1958).

PALMISTRY

Mahabal, Vernon. *The Secret Code on your Hands: An Illustrated Guide to Palmistry*. (San Rafael, CA: Mandala Publishing Group, 2000).

Mahabal, Vernon. Palmistry Cards. (Novato, CA: Mandala Publishing Group, 2002).

Hipskind, Judith. *Palmistry the Whole View* (St. Paul, Minnesota: Llewellyn Publications, 1998).

IRIS ANALYSIS

Johnson, Denny Ray. *What the Eye Reveals* (Boulder, CO: Rayid Publications, 1995).

BIRTH ORDER

Johnson, Denny and Edith Cuffe. *The Nature of Birth Order* (Mancos, CO: Rayid Publications, 2002).

ONLINE RESOURCES

METAPHYSICAL AND LIFE PURPOSE STUDIES

School of Intuitive Arts and Sciences http://www.schoolofintuitiveartsandsciences.org

PAST LIVES

Celestial Awakenings, http://www.celestialawakenings.com.

Susan Wisehart, http://www.susanwisehart.com.

Edgar Cayce Books World Database, http://www.edgarcayce.com.

IARRT, "International Association for Regression Research and Therapies, Inc.," http://www.iarrt.org.

Camp Chesterfield, http://www.Campchesterfield.com.

ARE, "Edgar Cayce's Association for Research and Enlightenment," http://www.edgarcayce.org.

Mediums, Inc., http://www.mediumsinc.com.

ASTROLOGY
AFA, "American Federation of Astrologers," http://www.astrologers.com.

Astro Communications Services, "AstroCom.com," http://www.astrocom.com.

NCGR, "National Council for Geocosmic Research, Inc.," http://www.geocosmic.org.
Friends of Astrology, http://www.friendsofastrology.org.

PALMISTRY
Vernon Mahabal, "The Palmistry Institute", <http://www.palmistryinstitute.com>

IRIS ANALYSIS
Rayid International, "The Rayid Place", http://www.rayid.com.

Dave Carpenter http://www.path-to-health.com.

Fergus and Trijntje Reilly, "Eyesite," http://www.cybersayer.com/eyesite.

Miles Research, "Miles Research," *The Rayid Model of Personality and Relationships*, http://www.milesresearch.com/main/aboutrayid.htm.

Miles Research, "Miles Research," *What Is Rayid?*, http://www.milesresearch.com/main/whatis.htm.

BIRTH ORDER
Rayid International, "The Rayid Place", http://www.rayid.com.

EDITORIAL SERVICES
Darlene Brill, Editor, D. Brill & Associates, Wheeling, Illinois.

ART DIRECTION, GRAPHIC DESIGN AND ILLUSTRATION
Debbie Mackall, Dimensions in Media, Inc.
24191 N. Forest Drive, Lake Zurich, IL 60047
debbie@dimensionsinmedia.com

Index

Pluto 20-23, 30, 38, 41, 48, 52, 135, 138-139
Psychic 105, 138
Pythagoras 54

Q

Quincunx 43

R

Rayid 1, 4, 77-79, 88-89, 91-92, 118, 125-127, 131, 133-142, 145, 149-150, 152, 154, 156, 158, 160, 162, 164, 179, 181, 183
Realistic 35
Receptive 20, 60, 85, 103, 106, 114, 118
Reincarnation 2, 9, 10
Right brain 85, 96, 133, 141, 142
Ring of Determination 86-87
Ring of Freedom 86-87
Ring of Harmony 86, 129, 133, 136, 139, 141
Ring of Purpose 86-87

S

Sagittarius 26, 31, 34, 38, 47, 126-128
Saturn 20-21, 24, 31, 38, 41-42, 51, 95, 97-98, 99-100, 103-104, 107, 110-111
Scorpio 25, 30, 34, 38, 48-49, 126-128, 138, 140
Semi-sextile 43
Sesquisquare 43
Sextile 43-44
Shaker 79-83, 90, 126-127, 130, 172
Shaker-Flower 80, 83, 172
Shaker-Jewel 80, 83
Sibling sequence 118
Soul 1, 4-6, 10-13, 15, 19, 22, 32, 45-46, 50, 54, 64-65, 70, 73-75, 78, 109, 114-115, 121, 123, 139, 177, 181, 195
South node 45-46, 139
Spatulate 100
Square 43, 95, 98, 100, 108-109
Stream 77, 79-84, 88-90, 92, 124
Stream-Flower 80, 84
Stream-Jewel 80, 83

Sun 17, 19-20, 24, 27, 29, 33, 37, 39-41, 43, 45, 48-49, 51, 98, 100, 104, 110, 126, 128-130, 135, 137-138, 140-142

T

Taurus 23-25, 27, 34, 37, 126-128
Trine 43-44

U

Uranus 20-22, 32, 38, 41, 50, 52, 137-138, 141

V

Venus 20, 24, 27, 30, 37-38, 40, 49, 51, 97-99, 102, 105, 111, 128, 134-138, 141, 180

About the Author

Kathryn Andries is the author of *Living Atlantis: My Year at the College of Metaphysics,* contributing author of *Interpreting Dreams for Self-Discovery*, and producer of the video *Inside the California Missions*. She earned a Bachelor of Arts degree from the University of Michigan, and a holistic health practitioner degree from Body Mind College in California. She has also completed extensive studies in the intuitive arts at the Berkeley Psychic Institute, the School of Metaphysics and the American Federation of Astrologers.

Ms. Andries has taught subjects ranging from foreign languages to health and spirituality in this country and abroad. She is a co-founder of the School of Intuitive Arts and Sciences where she teaches and lectures on the six methods of self-awareness, helping people to find their life mission and live their life to the fullest.

Acknowledgments

I want to thank all the teachers who led me on a path to discover my life purpose; Paulette Suzanne who taught me how to read the story in my eyes, Barry Green who showed me the mind-body connection, Pat Kelly who helped my intuitive abilities come alive, Terryll Nemeth who brought joy into metaphysics, Michelle Gobely for her astrological wisdom, and Connie and Bruce Compton for their insightful teachings and readings.

I am grateful for everyone who offered their advice and assistance in this project; Vernon Mahabal, Susan Wisehart, Jim Verghis, Michelle Gobely, Christine Arens, Dave Carpenter, Barbara Schermer, Jeanie Gold and Denny Johnson.

I appreciate everyone who made this book come alive with their personal stories; Sarah Wenning, Elaine Bentz, Jim Cerveny, Reid Reutell, Patrick Andries and Kathleen Beening.

Special thanks to Darlene Brill for her expert editorial services, and to Debbie Mackall for designing a cover that so perfectly reflects this material.

Extra special thanks to my husband Patrick for his computer expertise, and most importantly his love, support and encouragement.

ORDER FORM

I would like to order the following items:

_____Astrological chart *Include time, date, year, city, state/province, and country of birth*

_____Past life reading

_____Numerology profile *Include name as stated on the birth certificate, most recent last name, nicknames, and date and year of birth*

_____Iris photos and analysis

_____Palmistry reading *Include a photocopy of both palms.*

_____Family/birth order questionnaire and analysis

_____Comprehensive Life Purpose Analysis (includes all of the above)

Name_____ Phone _____

E-mail_____

Address_____

City_____State_____Zip_____

Send this form to **Kathryn Andries, P. O. Box 2071, Palatine, Illinois 60078**, or write to her at kathrynandries@aol.com to schedule an appointment.

Visit www.discoveryourlifepurpose.org for "Discover Your Life Purpose" class and workshop schedules, and "train the trainer" schedules.

To order additional copies of *Soul Choices: Six Paths to Find Your Life Purpose*, call BookMasters at 1-800-247-6553.